THE LANGUAGE ARTS IDEA BOOK

CLASSROOM ACTIVITIES FOR CHILDREN

GOODYEAR PUBLISHING COMPANY, INC.
SANTA MONICA, CALIFORNIA

JOANNE SCHAFF
READING CONSULTANT
MONROE, MICHIGAN PUBLIC SCHOOLS

THE LANGUAGE ARTS IDEA BOOK

CLASSROOM ACTIVITIES FOR CHILDREN

Schaff, Joanne.
    The language arts idea book.
    (Goodyear education series)
    1. Language arts (Elementary) 2. English language
—Study and teaching (Elementary) I. Title.
LB1576.S317   372.6′044   75-16597
ISBN 0-87620-519-8 (P)
ISBN 0-87620-520-1 (C)

Library of Congress Catalog Card Number: 75-16597
ISBN: 087620519-8
Y 5198-0
Current Printing (last number): 10 9
Printed in the United States of America

Supervising production editor, Sally Kostal
Copy editor, Janice Gallagher
Designer and art director, Louis Neiheisel
Co-designer and artist, Kitty Anderson
Signed art, Joanne Schaff

Teachers today continue to need creative ideas and activities to provide worthwhile experiences for children in the area of language arts. Many ideas used and reused by teachers over the years continue to fulfill an important role in teaching various concepts. New teachers seldom have the opportunity or time to visit many classrooms or to exchange the volume of new ideas which reside in their own minds with those creative ideas of experienced teachers. Hopefully, this collection of over three hundred activities will help fulfill that need. These special activities have been chosen with care to provide the teacher with experiences for children, which will arouse their interest, and create a stimulating environment for acquiring important language skills, knowledge, attitudes, and appreciation. Some of the activities were included to provide teachers with techniques and devices for helping children to listen and speak effectively and to write creatively. The activities can be used in any classroom environment, from the traditional arrangements to the rooms containing task groups, learning centers, and other individualized programs.

In order for the activities to be used effectively, the classroom should be a relaxed place, where children and the teacher can communicate and interact freely with one another. This kind of atmosphere is conducive to independent thinking and initiative on the part of the children. A variety of materials should be available and in the open for children to use independently for their ongoing projects. Bulletin boards should be changed and rearranged frequently by both the teacher and the children. Varied stimuli keep children's creative minds from becoming stifled and bored.

Many of the listening and oral language activities should be used by the teacher at the beginning of the school year, before attempting the creative writing. Some children are not as fluent or expressive as others, and any kind of writing at the start of school is often a painful experience. A few weeks later, after a great deal of oral exchange, brief writing experiences such as writing a caption or a descriptive phrase for a picture can pave the way for longer writing experiences. The shorter, simple activities are placed at the beginning of the creative writing section to act as building blocks toward the successful writing of stories. Overall, a teacher might begin the school year by using the techniques or activities that are more easily handled by the class. Then as the year progresses, activities can be chosen by the teacher which will best meet the needs of each individual child.

The grade levels found at the beginning of each activity are merely indicators of the most probable levels for using the ideas, but they could be used at other levels if a teacher deems them useful.

Most of the ideas contained in the book may be used as language extenders in conjunction with most of the newer basic reading series. Teachers will find additional activities to use with the readers in such areas as poetry writing (perhaps a limerick), word derivations, or games involving listening skills.

In recent years, developing a child's self-concept has gained an important

PREFACE

position in the classroom. Several activities projecting this concept are included for teachers.

The ideas and activities were collected or created over the past two decades. Much sorting, refining, and innovating was done in the process of creating the activities for this book. Many of the activities were developed while I taught in various grades from one through six, and while I was raising my own four children. Fellow teachers from Illinois, New York, Maryland, Florida, Michigan, and Ohio provided me with a few of their favorite techniques, devices, and ideas. They were collected on 3" by 5" cards, being constantly used by other teachers and myself. Student teachers, professors, and graduate students fulfilled a later role in providing me with new activities and an incentive to publish these ideas. Many teachers have expressed the need for such a book, and I feel that it can indeed be a useful tool.

Joanne Schaff

CONTENTS

CONTENTS

LISTENING

Grades 1–3
Getting Attention
with a Puppet

Using a hand puppet is an effective way to get children to listen. Have the children decide upon a name for the puppet. Each day the puppet could visit the class to describe an exciting happening, to read a school announcement, or to give some pencils, games, new plants, toys, or equipment for class use. As soon as the puppet appears on the teacher's hand, the children are ready to listen.

Grades 1–3
Summarizing
the Day's Events

A teacher can use a puppet at the end of the day to summarize important events or happenings. The puppet can praise many of the children for being good listeners or ask them what they have learned or what they have enjoyed most during the day.

Grades 1–6
Standards
for Listening

Encourage the class to develop (in class discussion) a list of standards for good listening. Record and display the list of standards in the room on colorful posterboard or large sheets of story paper. Some of the standards could be appropriately illustrated. You might start an illustrated poster with the phrase "Snoopy says . . ."

Grades 1–6
Listening to Poetry, Using Real Objects

Use and display real objects while reading a poem to the children. Place on a table bottles containing ground coffee, a sliced onion, a freshly cut apple, printer's ink, a piece of charred wood, tea, and a sprig of fir. After the poem ''Smells'' by Christopher Morley is read to the class, invite the children to sniff the various smells in the bottles.

The class can pop some popcorn while the teacher reads Laura Richards' poem ''The Song of the Corn-Popper.'' The poem will have special significance for the children if an automatic popper with a transparent cover is used so they can observe the kernels ''burst into warm white snow!''

Grades 3–5
Listening for Special Words

Ask the class to listen for the action words in a short taped poem. Write the action words in a column on the chalkboard. Replay the poem, asking the group to listen for words that create a picture in their minds. Write these words in another column. Then point to one of the descriptive words and ask, ''What could this word describe?'' For example:

Descriptive Words	Name Words	Action Words
beautiful	sunset	glowed
spotted	fawn	stared
huge	machine	rattled
delicate	rose	bloomed
sharp	knife	cut

Following this listening activity, the teacher can ask the class to create some sentences using the groups of words in each column.

Grades 1–6
Listening
for the Magic Word

Choose an unusual word to use sometime during the day. Use appropriate words for your students' grade level. Write the word in a corner of the chalkboard for the children to see. Instruct the class to listen for the word and, as soon as anyone hears it, to say, "Magic word." The student who hears it first will receive a special privilege for that day. A few interesting words to get you started are magenta, symptom, magpie, cucumber, eureka, antifreeze, quirk, and thud.

Grades 1–6
Discussing a
New Neighbor

Ask the children to listen while you read "The New Neighbor" by Rose Fyleman, from Brewton's *Gaily We Parade*. Initiate an active discussion by asking the children to think of questions *they* would ask a boy or girl their own age who is new in the neighborhood. Write the responses on an experience chart or chalkboard. Think of something nice or neighborly one could do for the new person. Arrange each new idea on a piece of oaktag cut to resemble the shape of the idea and place the pieces on a bulletin board.

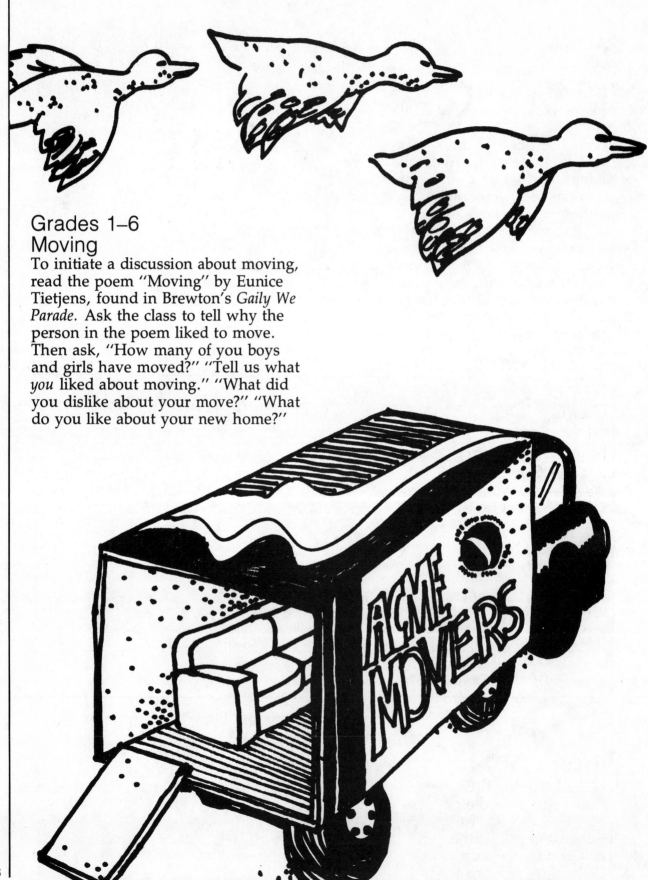

Grades 1–6
Moving

To initiate a discussion about moving, read the poem "Moving" by Eunice Tietjens, found in Brewton's *Gaily We Parade*. Ask the class to tell why the person in the poem liked to move. Then ask, "How many of you boys and girls have moved?" "Tell us what *you* liked about moving." "What did you dislike about your move?" "What do you like about your new home?"

Grades 3–6
"If I Had a
Hundred Dollars"

Ask the class to listen for the various ways for the child in the poem to spend his pennies as you read aloud "Penny Problem," by John Farrar, from Brewton's *Gaily We Parade*. List the possibilities on the chalkboard. Ask the class to think of other ways to spend four pennies. Say to the class, "Suppose you had a hundred dollars all your own. What would you do with it?" Then ask the children to write a paragraph or poem titled "If I Had a Hundred Dollars," explaining how and why they would spend the money.

Grades 1–6
Creating a Title

Read a poem to the class such as "Motor Cars" or "Rubber Boots" by Rowena Bastin Bennett and ask the children to make up a new title. Discuss the reasons for their choices.

Grades 3–5
Listening for Words
That Mean *Go*

Read several sentences to the class. Ask them to listen for words that mean *go* in each sentence and to write that word on their papers. Pause at the end of each sentence to give the children a chance to write the word. Use sentences such as the following: The car *zoomed* over the finish line to win the race. The wild ducks *flew* south for the winter. The baby *crawled* across the room to touch the kitten. The plane *disappeared* from sight. *Rowing* the boat across the river was such fun. The parachute jumper *plunged* through the air until his parachute unfolded to slow his descent. Let the children who are interested create sentences with action verbs.

Student Directions

Here Come the Whales!
by Alice Goudey

Read the questions on the cards that belong to the story and find the matching card containing the answer.

1. What kind of dangers did the whalemen face on their voyage?

Whalemen faced the dangers of shipwreck by storms, or running into icebergs in fog. Whales sometimes smashed a small boat to pieces.

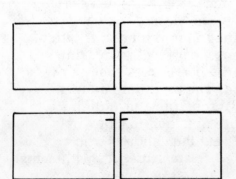

Answers are self-correcting by matching lines on back of cards.

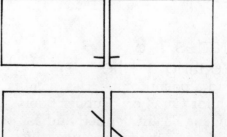

JS

Grades 3–6
Listening for Facts

Tape-record an informative book or article relating to a unit of study. Ask a student to listen carefully (on earphones) for facts brought out by the material. Prior to the activity, construct ten question cards and ten answer cards, about the material, on separate 3″ x 5″ white index cards. Ask the student to match a question card with the correct answer card. The teacher can make the cards self-correcting by using matching lines on the back of the cards. This activity is very appealing to children.

Grades 3–5
Listening to a Story

After reading a story to the class about a child with strong personal characteristics (such as the story about Homer Price, by Robert McClosky), have each child write his reasons for wanting Homer Price as a friend.

Grades 3–5
Telling Reasons Why

After the class has viewed a movie or listened to material about Japan or another foreign country, ask them to write a paragraph explaining why each person would (or would not) enjoy living in Japan. Ask them to draw an appropriate illustration.

Grades 1–3
Tape-recording Stories

Have the children tape-record their own stories. Play the stories for groups of five or six children. Follow the listening session with a good discussion by each small group of children.

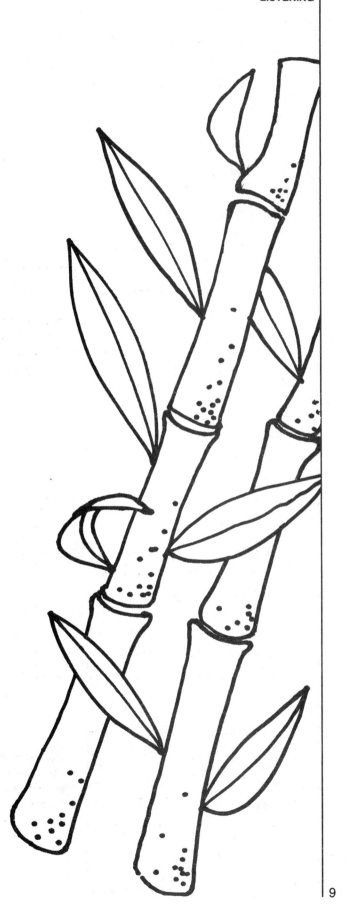

Grades 1–5
Solving Riddles

After completing a unit of study, ask the class to write the answer to some riddles you have developed. For instance, if the unit completed is about the circus, ask your first graders to name and draw the animal that the riddle describes. Perhaps a fourth-grade class has just finished a geography unit. Describe, in detail, geographical areas studied and have the class tell the names of the areas. At the end of each circus-animal description, ask, "Who Am I?" At the end of each geographical description, ask, "What Am I Describing?"

Grades 4–6
Listening for Key Words

Ask the class to listen carefully as you read an informative article about a specific area you are studying. Write several key words or unusual vocabulary words on the chalkboard to help the students remember what they heard. Then ask them to write everything they can remember from their listening. Award a point for each fact remembered.

Grades 3–5
Listening for Details

Read the story "The Two Stonecutters" by Eve Titus to the class. Ask them to listen for three wishes. Discuss the wishes and their consequences, then ask the children to write, "If I had three wishes . . ." The story can be found in *Children's Digest*, February 1969, and is also in book form.

Grades 4–5
Determining What
Will Come Next

Read a short paragraph, perhaps from a recent news story, to the class. Stop in the middle of a sentence or at a critical point in the paragraph and have the children determine what will come next. Individualize the activity by audio-taping the story and setting up a listening post for a small task group of three or four children.

Grades 1–3
Beginning Sounds of Words

Ask the class to listen for the two sounds at the *beginning* of *st*ep. If they hear this sound, ask them to clap once: stem, some, bank, steep, sleep, stop, stir, skip, past, staple, steeple.

Grades 1–3
Clapping Your Hands

Read a paragraph or a story to a group of children, asking them to clap their hands:

(a) when they hear the name of an animal. Use *My Easy-to-Read True Book of Animal Babies* by Illa Podendorf;

(b) whenever they hear a word that describes something. Use "Hide and Seek Fog" by Alvin Tresselt;

(c) every time they hear a word that names something. Use "The Little House" by Virginia Lee Burton; or

(d) when they hear a word that begins (or ends) with a certain sound, such as *b*.

Grades 1–2
Listening for Sounds

Have the class listen to sounds outside the classroom. Discuss what they hear outside the window and what they hear in the hallway. Then ask the children what they might hear in their mothers' kitchens. Have the children fold a piece of drawing paper into four sections and draw pictures of the sounds they heard in the house just before they got ready for school.

Grades 1–3
Making a Sounds Map

Take the children for a walk around the school to listen to all the sounds around them. Upon returning to the classroom, tape a large piece of colored paper to the chalkboard and draw a map of the area covered on your field trip. With the help of the children's oral comments, pinpoint locations on the map and write the sounds heard there.

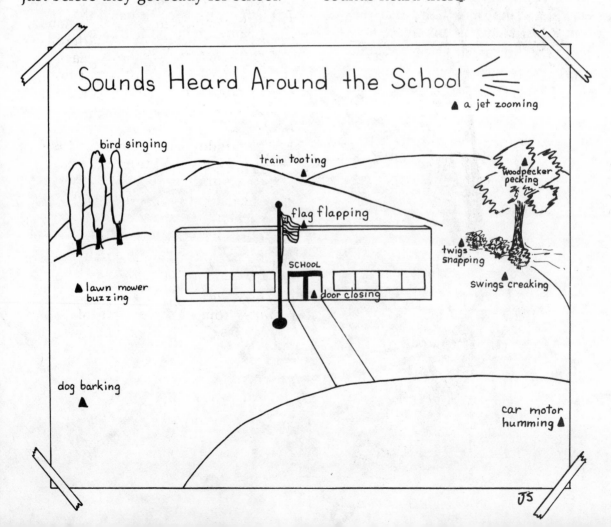

Sounds Heard Around the School

▲ a jet zooming

bird singing

train tooting ▲

woodpecker pecking ▲

flag flapping

SCHOOL

twigs snapping ▲

▲ lawn mower buzzing

door closing ▲

swings creaking ▲

dog barking ▲

car motor humming ▲

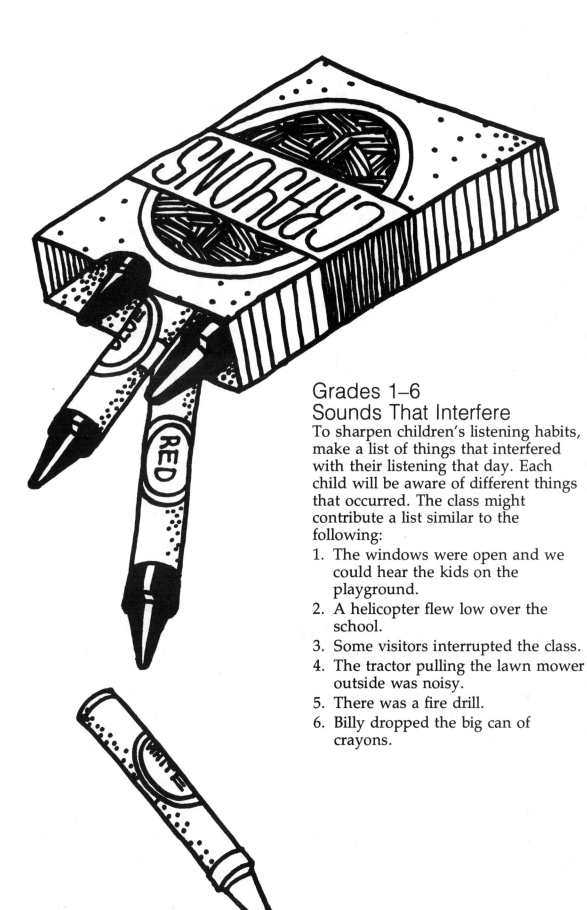

Grades 1–6
Sounds That Interfere

To sharpen children's listening habits, make a list of things that interfered with their listening that day. Each child will be aware of different things that occurred. The class might contribute a list similar to the following:

1. The windows were open and we could hear the kids on the playground.
2. A helicopter flew low over the school.
3. Some visitors interrupted the class.
4. The tractor pulling the lawn mower outside was noisy.
5. There was a fire drill.
6. Billy dropped the big can of crayons.

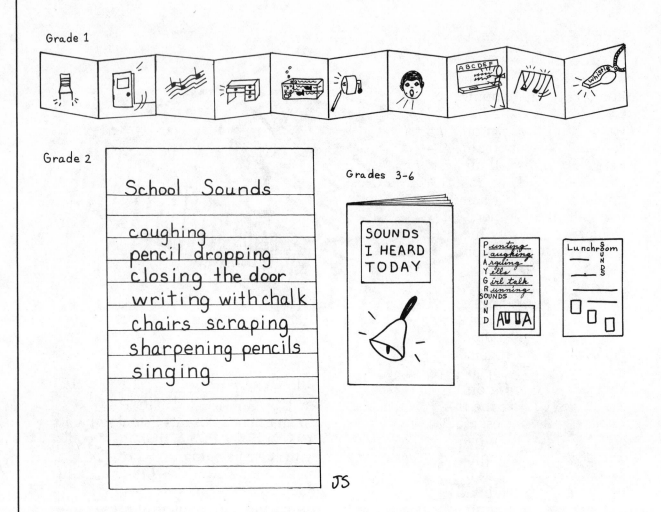

Grade 1

Grade 2

School Sounds

coughing
pencil dropping
closing the door
writing with chalk
chairs scraping
sharpening pencils
singing

Grades 3-6

SOUNDS
I HEARD
TODAY

Punting
Laughing
Arguing
Yells
Girl talk
Running
SOUNDS

AUJA

Lunchroom
SOUNDS

JS

Grades 1–6
Listening for Daytime Sounds

Have the children keep a record over a one-day period of all the sounds that they can remember. The younger children could draw a sequence of pictures. Enlist a group of fourth, fifth, or sixth graders to make a collection of sounds heard over the weekend. They might cut pictures from magazines, draw the source of the sounds for a bulletin board, or make interesting illustrated booklets and posters.

Grades 1–2
Listening to Noises

Ask the children to close their eyes and listen very carefully to several kinds of sounds. Have them tell you the various noises they heard, such as paper being ripped, a line being drawn with a piece of chalk across the chalkboard, footsteps, a sneeze, and the sound of a zipper being closed. Let a group of four or five children choose some noises and present them to the class. They might present their sounds from behind the piano, a divider, or the teacher's desk while the listeners keep their eyes open.

Grades 1–3
Identifying Taped Sounds

Tape-record sounds such as a horn honking, paper ripping, a cuckoo clock sounding the hour, a bucket of water being thrown on the grass, someone walking, someone running, a dog scratching, thunder booming, a child roller-skating, raindrops falling on the window, or someone clearing the table after dinner. Ask the children to identify these sounds.

Tape sounds in groups such as kitchen noises: a faucet dripping; a dishwasher running; a refrigerator ice-maker producing ice cubes; someone placing dishes in the cupboard, placing utensils on the table, or slicing vegetables; an electric mixer whirring; popcorn crackling; or someone switching on lights, moving a table, or closing the front door. Tape outside noises: a police siren shrieking, the lawn being mowed, a woodpecker pecking, a group of boys playing basketball or baseball, trucks driving by, the sprinkler swishing, the ice-cream man ringing his bell, or rugs being shaken. Allow the children to tape some sounds at home and share them with their classmates at school.

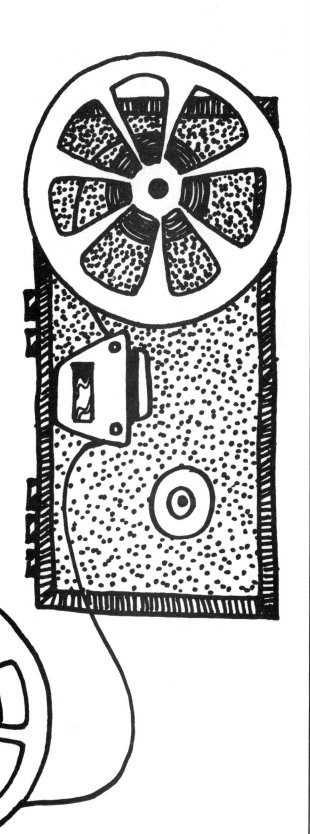

Grades K–1
Using Mother
Goose Rhymes

Mother Goose rhymes can be used effectively by the teacher as a listening activity. As the teacher reads a poem, the children can pantomime the action. Explain to the children that they must listen carefully in order to pantomime. There are numerous Mother Goose rhymes to use:

- "Little Bo-Peep"
- "Robin Redbreast"
- "Little Boy Blue"
- "The Clever Hen"
- "Wee Willie Winkie"
- "Simple Simon"
- "A Little Man"
- "Little Jack Horner"
- "Dance Thumbkin, Dance" (Use thumb and fingers)
- "A Candle"
- "Miss Muffet"
- "Humpty Dumpty"
- "Old Mother Hubbard"
- "Jack and Jill"
- "The Mulberry Bush"
- "The Old Woman and the Peddler"
- "The Tarts"

Grades 1–6
Listening to Description

Read a description of a scene to the class, then ask the children to draw pictures from the information they heard. After everyone has exchanged pictures, reread the description, giving one point for each object represented in the completed pictures.

Grades 1–5
Listening to Mood Music

Play some mood music, while the children draw, paint, or fingerpaint pictures that the music impresses upon their minds. Some suitable and favorite selections are Tchaikovsky's "Nutcracker Suite," "Sleeping Beauty Ballet," and "Swan Lake"; "Slavonic Dances" and selected sections of "New World Symphony" by Dvořák; Grieg's "Peer Gynt Suite"; "William Tell Overture" and "Dance of the Hours" by Rossini; selected sections of "Petrouchka" by Stravinsky; "Grand Canyon Suite" by Grofé; "La Mer" by Debussy; and "Till Eulenspiegel" by R. Strauss.

Grades 1–6
Listening to a Poem,
Creating a Picture

Ask the children to listen carefully to
a poem you will read to them, then
have them create a scene or picture
about the poem. There are many
poems to choose from for this activity.
For grades 1-2, the *Anthology of
Children's Literature* by Johnson, Scott,
and Sickels, contains the poems
"Skyscrapers," "Taxis," "General
Store," and "Roads," all written by
Rachel Field; "Windy Wash Day" and
"Hiding" by Dorothy Aldis; "My
Shadow" and "Block City" by Robert
Louis Stevenson. Print the poem on
an experience chart and display it
along with the children's drawings.
Children in grades 3 through 6 might
enjoy working in groups to create a
panorama, on long sheets of white
paper, describing Eleanor Farjeon's
"The Sounds in the Morning."

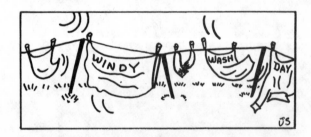

Grades 1–6
Creating Interest
in New Books

Each week or two the teacher, with a committee of three of four children, should choose fifty or sixty books from the school library for the free reading shelf in the classroom. Skim through several of these books and place bookmarks in places where there is an exciting incident, a beautiful description, an interesting illustration, a humorous section, or an exciting buildup for a mystery. Point out and read from these selections each day to interest the children in reading the books.

Grades 1–3
Listening to Each Other

During show-and-tell time, have the children gather in groups of six, each group deciding upon a new leader for the day. Change the groups each week. Ask the children to share an interesting object or piece of information with the group.

Grades 3–6
Collecting Poems

Encourage children to cut out or copy poems from books or magazines. Give the children time each day to read these to the class. Interested class members can organize these collections and make them into booklets, keep them in manila envelopes or folders, paste them into a classroom poetry scrapbook, or keep them in shoeboxes. Give the poetry committee the responsibility of creating headings or categories for their collection of poems. Be sure to include poems written by the children.

Grades 1–2
Listening to a Paragraph, Dramatizing

Read a paragraph about an animal from a unit of study. Tell the class to listen carefully so that someone can pretend to be the animal and act out the paragraph. For example: The mother robin pecked at the soft grass and snatched a fat, juicy worm. She looked cautiously to the left, then to the right. Quickly flying up to her nest, she placed the worm right into the open mouth of the nearest baby robin.

Grades 3–6
Paying Attention: Short Talks and Secret Signals

Ask a few children to present short talks on any subject of interest to each individual. Explain that they may have to speak under difficult circumstances that are being planned. Tell them to keep talking no matter what anyone in the class may do. Following this explanation, ask the speakers to leave the room. Then tell the class to be good listeners until they are given a secret signal from you, which might be a wink, a cough, or a glance out the window. The class should stop paying attention after the signal is given and start drawing on pieces of paper, look out the windows, read books silently, start coughing or laughing, or put their heads on their desks. After this short planning session, ask one of the speakers to come back into the room and start his talk. After they have all completed their talks, ask how each felt when the class was not paying attention. Continue the discussion by focusing on the class's responsibility to listen when someone is speaking to them.

Grades 1–3
Telling Stories Using
Pantomime and Sounds

Ask the children to make up stories. Instead of telling the stories with words, the students will tell them with sounds, perhaps adding some pantomime. A small group of children might work up a story together. Here is a story made up by a first-grade girl: A girl sat in a chair pretending to read a book. She heard the sound of a bell in the distance and looked out the window. She opened the door, ran outside to the curb and waved her hand. She produced some jingling coins, traded them for an ice-cream cone, and started licking it.

Grades 1–5
Listening to Poems,
Pantomiming

There are unlimited numbers of poems that can serve as a listening activity. Following a poetry reading, let the children pantomime the characters in the poem. Some poems that are especially appropriate are "The Animal Store" by Rachel Field, "Casey at the Bat" by Ernest Thayer, "The Grasshoppers" and "Hiding" by Dorothy Aldis, "If I Were a Little Pig" by Lucy Sprague, "Around the Corner," "Out in the Rain," "Shore," and "Fat Old Witch" by Leland Jacobs, "The Song of the Corn-Popper" by Laura Richards, "The Duel" by Eugene Field, and "Jonathan Bing" by Beatrice Curtis Brown.

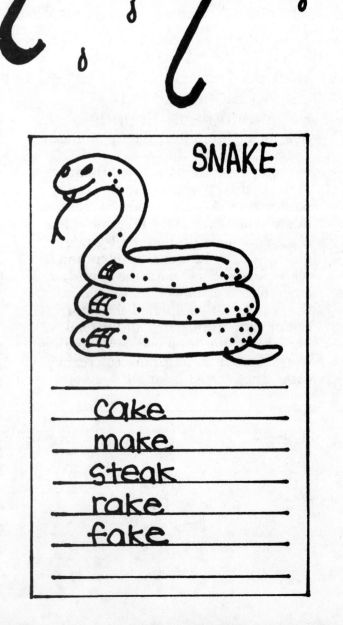

Grades 1–4
Listening for Word Sounds
Have the children listen for words from poems read to them that make them hear sounds—dashing, rolling, laughing, whirring, buzzing, etc. Use poems such as "The Umbrella Brigade" by Laura Richards, "Chairoplane Chant" by Nancy Byrd Turner, "Wild Beasts" by Evaleen Stein, and "Circus" and "The Sounds in the Morning" by Eleanor Farjeon. All of these poems can be found in *Anthology of Children's Literature* by Johnson, Scott, and Sickels. Make a list of these word sounds on the chalkboard as they are contributed by each child. Display such lists on story paper for third and fourth graders so they can use these words in their creative writing.

Grades 1–2
Making Sounds
Ask the children to make up word sounds for various animals (dog, cow, horse, bear, etc.); sad sounds, happy sounds; sounds of rain, thunder, lightning, hail, snow, and wind; an airplane, a jet, a boat, and a fire engine. To introduce this activity read the poems "A Rain Song" by Clinton Scollard or "Now the Noisy Winds Are Still" by Mary Mapes Dodge. Have the children make the sounds of the rain, the wind, the brook, the birds' song, and the crisp old leaves mentioned in the poems as you read them.

SNAKE

cake
make
steak
rake
fake

Grades 1–3
Rhyming Animal Names

Ask the children to think of the name of an animal, then choose a word that rhymes with it. Your list may look something like this:

dog	log	skunk	_____
cat	bat	porcupine	_____
horse	force	otter	_____
bat	hat	squirrel	_____
owl	fowl	bear	_____
cow	_____	monkey	_____
pig	_____	elephant	_____
snake	_____	giraffe	_____
frog	_____	camel	_____
toad	_____	swan	_____

The class might cut pictures of animals from magazines and paste them on construction paper. Record animal names and several rhyming words under the picture.

OWL

fowl
growl
howl

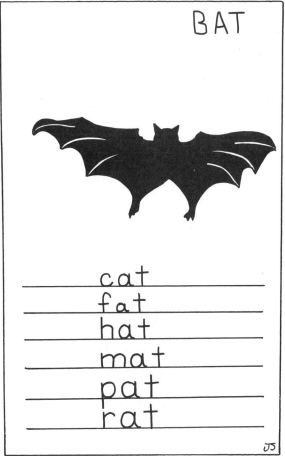

BAT

cat
fat
hat
mat
pat
rat

Grades 4–6
Interviewing

Ask each member of the class to interview someone, perhaps a parent, grandparent, neighbor, teacher, or friend, about a special interest or hobby. Following the interviews, discuss with the class the various facets of learning by this method. Compare interviewing to reading or watching TV. Record the points as they are mentioned, either on the chalkboard or on story paper.

Grades 5–6
Listening to News
Broadcasts

Tape-record a five-minute radio or TV news report that states only facts. Then record a newscast by a news commentator who presents his opinions of the news. After the class has listened to the two different styles of news, ask the class to share their opinions about the differences between the tapes. Ask the class or a small group to write a paragraph describing the differences between the two news presentations. This activity can also be set up for individual listening on earphones.

Grades 1–6
Identifying Famous
People from Descriptions

Read descriptions of people the class is studying and ask the class members to guess their names. For example, describe George Washington to a first- or second-grade class by saying, "This great man was a general, the first president of the United States, and built a home called Mt. Vernon." Older students in grades 3 through 6 could develop their own descriptions, collect them in a shoebox, then proceed to play the game. Divide the class into two or three groups. The group identifying the most people wins the game.

Grades 1–6
Listening to TV
Programs for Details

Children spend a great deal of time watching TV. Plan structured listening experiences for the class such as the following: (1) Watch "How the Grinch Stole Christmas" tonight to see if the story is interpreted as it is written in this book by Dr. Seuss that I am reading to you today. (2) Watch "A Christmas Carol" tonight on TV. Note any additions, changes, or omissions as compared to the story I read to you by Dickens. (3) Watch the Hall of Fame play, "The Small Miracle." Find out if the orphaned Italian boy finds help for his ailing donkey. (4) Watch "A Threatened Paradise" on TV. Find out how Florida may be threatened by the same kind of environmental pollution suffered by so many of our northern states. In class we will explore its causes and its possible cures. (5) A *National Geographic* Special on TV will explore "The Old West" as it is today. Please watch it at 7:30 this evening. In class we will discuss what we learned about the West in the 1800s and compare the Old West with what it has become now.

Grades 1–6
Creating Chain Stories

Start an eventful story, then choose a child to continue it from the point at which you stop. Give several children the opportunity to add to the story. As the children progress through the chain of events, tape the story. They will enjoy hearing the completed version as it is replayed.

Grades 1–3
"Upset the Fruit Basket" Variations

Variation 1: When the children are becoming acquainted at the beginning of the year, list each child's name on the chalkboard. The child who is It calls the names of two children who try to exchange seats quickly. It tries to get into one of the vacated seats. The person remaining without a seat is It. Occasionally It might shout "fly away" instead of "upset the fruit basket," and everyone must exchange seats.

Variation 2: On Halloween, ask each child to choose a Halloween name, then list it on the board. Exchange seats when two Halloween names are called. "Ride the broomstick" may be the signal for the class to jump up and find another seat.

Variation 3: During Thanksgiving week make a list of the many kinds of foods the children might see on their Thanksgiving tables. Assign the name of a food to each child. When the names of two foods are called, the two children assigned to those names exchange seats. "Turkey's trot" will signal all the children to exchange seats.

Grades 1–6
Making a Sentence

A child or the teacher can start the game by saying a word such as "an." That child should call on a classmate to provide another word to add to the first, perhaps "an elephant." Another designated child might add "an elephant lifted," and so on until a child is unable to repeat the sequence of words accurately or to add a sensible word.

Grades 1–6
Guessing the Secret Place

Play the listening game "Guess the Secret Place" by having the children listen to the directions a teacher or a child gives to a certain spot in the room, school, or community. Let the individual who correctly guesses the secret place give directions to a new spot.

Grades 1–5
Following Directions, Sequence

Divide the class into four groups. Award a point to each group for following directions perfectly. Give each child a specific direction or sequence of directions to follow, for example: Take off your right shoe, put it on the top of your desk, put it on again, and take one hop. You might ask the next child to count to 10, open the classroom door, get a drink, and close the door. Another example: Pick up the paper under your desk, throw it in the corner wastebasket, turn to page 24 in your reader, and read the second paragraph. Another example: Write the number 10 on the chalkboard, divide it by 5, and add 12 to your answer.

Bring my
sailboat, pan,
yardstick,
stocking cap,
and flashlight.

Grades 1–3
Treasure Chest

Place many simple, familiar objects in a box labeled *Treasure Chest*. Ask a child to be King. The King says, "Bring my _____, _____, _____, _____, _____, naming several things in the box. The King chooses a child to bring him items from the chest. If the child he chooses gets all the items mentioned, that child becomes King.

Grades 1–2
"I Found Something"
The teacher can start the game by saying, "I found something." Describe the object and have the children guess what it is. Whoever guesses correctly gets to be It.

Grades 1–3
"I'm Going on a Trip"
In order to play the listening game "I'm Going on a Trip" say, "I'm going on a trip and will take a kite." The next player repeats the previous player's word and adds one that contains a long *i* sound such as *light*. Continue in this manner until a child is unable to repeat the sequence of words in order or does not give a long *i* word. Vary the game by using only words containing long *o* sounds, short *e* sounds, etc., or use words that begin or end with the same sound. A few examples are: "I'm going on a trip and will take a *strap* (*star*, *stick*, *store*, *stair*, *steeple*)." "I'm going on a trip and will take a wrea*th* (ba*th*, pa*th*, clo*th*)." "I'm going on a trip and will take a *trombone* (*trumpet*, *tray*, *track* suit, *tree*)."

BIBLIOGRAPHY:
Part One

Brewton, John. *Gaily We Parade.* New York: The Macmillan Company, 1940.
Poems–"Moving," Eunice Tietjens
    "The New Neighbor," Rose Fyleman
    "Penny Problem," John Farrar

————. *Under the Tent of the Sky.* New York: The Macmillan Company, 1937.
Poems–"The Animal Store," Rachel Field
    "The Grasshoppers," Dorothy Aldis

Burton, Virginia Lee. *The Little House.* Boston: Houghton Mifflin Company, 1942.

Dickens, Charles. *A Christmas Carol.* New York: The Macmillan Company, 1950.

Geismer, Barbara Peck. *Very Young Verses.* Boston: Houghton Mifflin Company, 1945.
Poem–"If I Were a Little Pig," Lucy Sprague

Jacobs, Leland. *Just Around the Corner.* New York: Holt, Rinehart, and Winston, 1964.
Poems–"Around the Corner"
    "Out in the Rain"
    "Shore"
    "Fat Old Witch"

Johnson, Edna; Scott, Carrie E.; and Sickels, Evelyn R. *Anthology of Children's Literature.* Boston: Houghton Mifflin Company, 1970.
Poems–"The Song of the Corn-Popper," Laura Richards
    "Smells," Christopher Morley
    "Motor Cars" and "Rubber Boots," Rowena Bastin Bennet
    Mother Goose Rhymes

    "Skyscrapers," "Taxis," "General Store," and "Roads," Rachel Field
    "Windy Wash Day" and "Hiding," Dorothy Aldis
    "My Shadow" and "Block City," Robert Louis Stevenson
    "The Sounds of the Morning" and "Circus," Eleanor Farjeon
    "The Duel," Eugene Field
    "Jonathan Bing," Beatrice Curtis Brown
    "The Umbrella Brigade," Laura Richards
    "Chairoplane Chant," Nancy Byrd Turner
    "Wild Beasts," Evaleen Stein
    "A Rain Song," Clinton Scollard
    "Now the Noisy Winds Are Still," Mary Mapes Dodge

McClosky, Robert. *Homer Price.* New York: Viking Press, 1943.

Podendorf, Illa. *My Easy-to-Read True Book of Animal Babies.* New York: Grosset & Dunlap, Inc., 1955.

The Real Mother Goose. Chicago: Rand McNally & Company, 1944.

Seuss, Dr. *How the Grinch Stole Christmas.* New York: Random House, Inc., 1957.

Thayer, Ernest. *Casey at the Bat.* New York: Franklin Watts, Inc., 1964.

Titus, Eve. *The Two Stonecutters.* Garden City, New York: Doubleday & Company, Inc., 1967.

Tresselt, Alvin. *Hide and Seek Fog.* New York: Lothrop, Lee, & Shepard Company, Inc., 1965.

2
SPEAKING

Grades 3–6
Discussing Proverbs

At the beginning of each new week of school, write or post a proverb in a special place in the classroom. Discuss the proverb's meaning with the class, and ask the children to see if its meaning affects any of them during the week. At the end of the week, discuss specific examples of how the proverb influenced anyone in the class. Some proverbs that can effectively be used in the classroom are:

- Keep conscience clear, then never fear.
- Make haste slowly.
- Haste makes waste.
- Be slow in choosing a friend, slower in changing.
- Three may keep a secret if two of them are dead.
- Well done is better than well said.
- A true friend is the best possession.
- You may delay, but time will not.
- The doors of wisdom are never shut.
- Well done is twice done. (The nine preceding proverbs are by Benjamin Franklin.)
- A soft answer turneth away wrath. (Bible)
- The only way to have a friend is to be one. (Ralph Waldo Emerson)
- When angry, count to ten before you speak; if very angry, a hundred. (Thomas Jefferson)
- Everything has its beauty but not everyone sees it. (Confucius)
- Beauty is truth, truth beauty. . . . (John Keats)

- A good book is the best of friends, the same today and forever. (Martin Tupper)
- Some books are to be tasted, others to be swallowed, and some few to be chewed and digested. (Francis Bacon)
- A little learning is a dangerous thing. (Alexander Pope)
- Honesty is the best policy. (Old English Proverb)
- Knowledge is power. (Thomas Hobbes)
- It is not how long, but how well we live. (John Ray)
- Many hands make light work. (John Heywood)
- The sweetest of all sounds is praise. (Xenophon)
- In sleep we are all equal. (Old Spanish Proverb)
- All's well that ends well. (John Heywood)
- Two heads are better than one. (John Heywood)

Grades 1–2
Creating a
Surprise Box

Suggest to the class that they might enjoy sharing certain possessions with the rest of the class for a day. The possession should be something very special to that person, perhaps a smooth, shiny rock, a music box, a lovely picture created at home, or a batch of cookies the child made. Let the child choose the day he wishes to bring something for the surprise box. When the day arrives, the child will secretly place the object in the box. During sharing time, the child can describe the object and ask the class to guess what it is. After three guesses, the child will make the object appear from the box. There are times when the teacher can share a special thing with the class such as an invitation to a play, a box of new pencils, or a new library book.

Grades 1–6
Conversing

At the start of the school year, converse a great deal with the children; share feelings about many things. For instance:
1. Tell us about your pet or a pet you would like.
2. What did you do after school yesterday?
3. What do you and your friends like to do together?

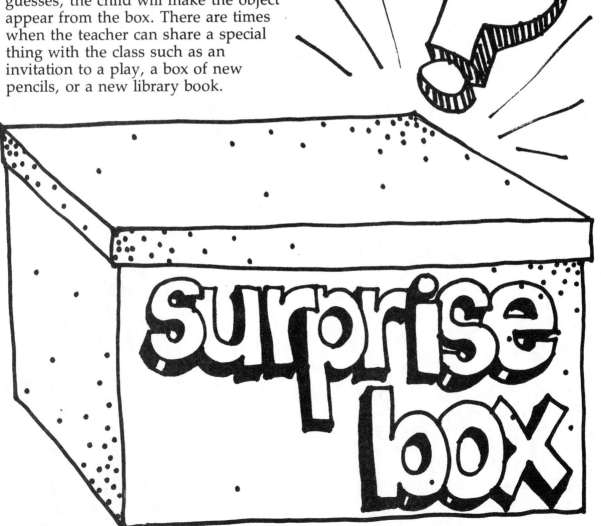

Grades 1–6
Solving the
Problem of "Don't"

After reading the poem "I Don't Like Don't—I Don't, I Don't" by Lucia and James L. Hymes, Jr., encourage a class discussion by asking the children what parents, brothers, sisters, and teachers forbid them to do. Ask them how to solve the problem of hearing "Don't." (The poem can be found under Pet Peeves on page 162.)

Grades 3–6
Exploring Self-concepts

Encourage a class discussion around the following statements: Tell what kind of person you think you are; explain the kind of person your friends and family think you are. Follow this discussion with a creative writing activity. Ask the children to write a sentence or a paragraph describing how they see themselves.

Grades 1–3
Discussing Fears

After orally reading the story "How to Scare a Lion" by Dorothy Stephenson, ask the class what Fearless Frederick's greatest fear was (Leonard's hiccups) and how he handled it. Change the discussion to children's fears, and ask them if they have ever been afraid of something. Accept as many responses as possible. Discuss alternatives for resolving their fears. The teacher can tell about a fear he or she may have harbored in the past and explain how the problem was solved.

Splat! went the egg as it hit the floor instead of the pan.

The deep, low "grrrr" of the German shepherd kept us from entering the yard.

Swish bang, swish bang went Tippy's tail against the sliding glass door, as the kids petted the big sheep dog.

I heard the crunch of twigs and dry leaves as we hiked through the woods.

Grades 2–5
Building a Sentence from Sounds

Put sounds on cards, pass one to each class member, then ask the children to build orally a sentence or short story around the cards. Use such sounds as boom, crrunch, shhhh, grrrr, ouch, ugh, ooo-ooo-ooo, heehaw, splat, chirp chirp, swish bang swish bang, rat-a-tat-tat, and others. Children enjoy listening to each other's sentences and stories.

The oil tank exploded with a deafening BOOM!

We heard the mother robin say chirp, chirp to her baby.

"Shhh! Your brother is sick today, so turn the TV down," said Mother.

Debbie squealed Ouch! as she pricked her finger on a rose bush.

JS

In my opinion...

Grades 3–6
Expressing Opinions

Give the children the opportunity to express their opinions on certain topics written on strips of paper and placed in a shoebox. Let each child choose a strip of paper. Some possible topics are:

- I am really happy when . . .
- I feel angry when . . .
- The best thing that ever happened to me was . . .
- I like . . .
- I don't like . . .
- I want to be _____ when I grow up. (Explain why.)
- My favorite book is _____ because . . .
- My favorite TV program is _____ because . . .
- The kind of bike I would like is . . .
- My favorite food is . . .
- My favorite football (or basketball) team is _____ because . . .
- One time I lost my . . .
- I would like to visit _____ because . . .

Grades 3–6
Choosing and
Discussing a Topic

Ask the class to place their chairs in a circle or square, then choose and discuss one of the topics listed on a large sheet of oaktag. The following choices can be used many times:

- The day I missed the bus
- The best meal I ever ate
- The worst storm I ever saw
- The nicest person I have ever met
- The most difficult thing that I have done
- My most depressing day
- The first time I went skiing (surfing, ice skating)
- What I like about my best friend
- The most amusing moment I've had
- How to be a good parent
- What I would do with a thousand dollars
- My most embarrassing moment
- My most enjoyable vacation
- A problem that is bothering me
- My favorite dessert
- The most memorable event of this week
- My favorite game
- Moments of disappointment
- Things I like to do
- Places I like to go
- My favorite sport
- The most exciting day I have ever had
- The funniest thing I've ever seen
- My lucky day

Grades 3–6
Discussing Word Meanings

Discuss what the word *success* means, then record on an experience chart what children think success is. One group might contribute these impressions:

Success is

- getting my boots on
- getting all my words correct on the spelling test
- saving enough money to buy a ten-speed bike
- winning a game of Monopoly

Try this activity using other words such as kindness, failure, mischief, distress, and gratification.

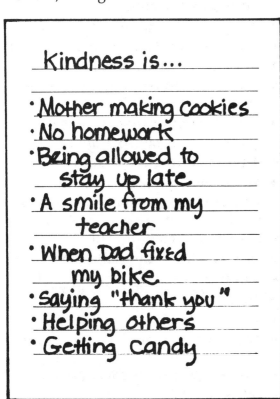

Kindness is...

· Mother making cookies
· No homework
· Being allowed to
    stay up late
· A smile from my
    teacher
· When Dad fixed
    my bike
· Saying "thank you"
· Helping others
· Getting candy

Distress is...

· Being cold
· Getting wet
· Breaking a leg
· Having a cinder
    in my eye
· Having a
    stomach ache
· Being hungry
· Losing a dollar
· Eating spinach
· A too hot day

Grades 1–5
Discussing Picture Book Stories

A beautiful picture book without text, called *The Silver Pony* by Lynd Ward, is a useful tool for the teacher. The book is a collection of eighty pictures that tell a story. Use the book with four or five children and have them discuss and describe what is happening in the pictures. To motivate oral expression about the illustrations, ask such questions as:

- What is the boy thinking?
- What is going to happen?
- What will the boy do?
- What is the boy's name?

Ask the children to tell the story of each picture. The illustrations can be displayed with an opaque projector for a large group discussion.

Grades 1–6
Storytelling from a Picture

Using interesting pictures mounted on bright construction paper, ask a child to pick one, then use it to tell a story to a small group of three or four children. The child should look at the picture and tell what is occurring, explain the circumstances that led to the events in the picture, then think of a story ending. Explain to the children that they can be as imaginative as they wish, and suggest that the story be as realistic or as fanciful as possible.

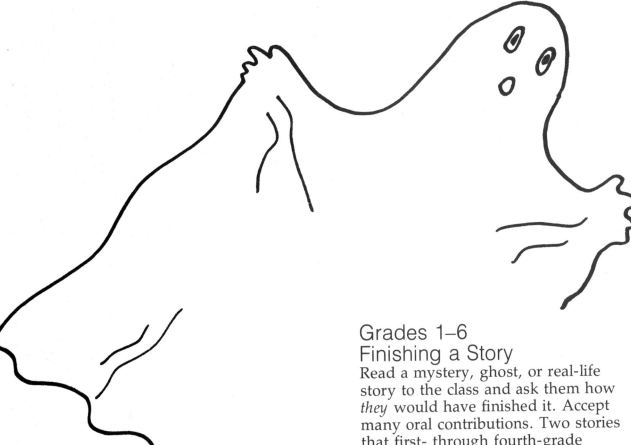

Things to Do on a Boring Day

Make some playdough. Be a sculptor.
Start a leaf collection.
Make some fudge with a friend.
Polish some furniture.
Call three friends. Play a game.
Make a papier-maché mask.
Clean out your closet. Paint it.
Make a soap carving.
Cut material scraps into squares,
sew them together, make a quilt.
Plan a picnic with a friend.
Go to the library. Find a good book.

Grades 1–6
Finishing a Story

Read a mystery, ghost, or real-life story to the class and ask them how *they* would have finished it. Accept many oral contributions. Two stories that first- through fourth-grade children especially enjoy at Halloween time are Jane Thayer's "What's a Ghost Going To Do?" and Mary Calhoun's "The Witch of Hissing Hill." Two or three fifth and sixth graders could create their own story for the class to finish orally.

Grades 1–6
Planning Creative Amusements

Ask each child to use his imagination and think of at least one way a child his age could entertain himself on a boring day. Record these ideas on an experience chart or the chalkboard. A few schemes might include making cookies or fudge, building a shelf for games, tightening all the loose screws on light switches and outlets, polishing the furniture, making a papier-maché mask, calling your friends over for a game of Clue, or making a ski jump in the backyard.

Grades 1–6
Creating a Tone Poem

Create a tone poem for Parents' Night Open House. Tape-record the children's voices as each identifies himself and makes comments on the topic "What my parents mean to me." Choose some pleasant music to play as a background for the children's voices, perhaps a recording of piano music by Chopin or the Overture to Tannhäuser by Wagner. Vary the music and topics for other special occasions.

Grades 1–3
Imagining Magic Objects

Ask the children to bring an object to school in a small box. Read them a story about something magic, such as "Longbeard the Wizard" by Fleischman or "Sylvester and the Magic Pebble" by William Steig. Discuss the magic in the story. Suggest that the children imagine a way for the object in their boxes to perform some kind of magic for them. Give each child the opportunity to share his idea.

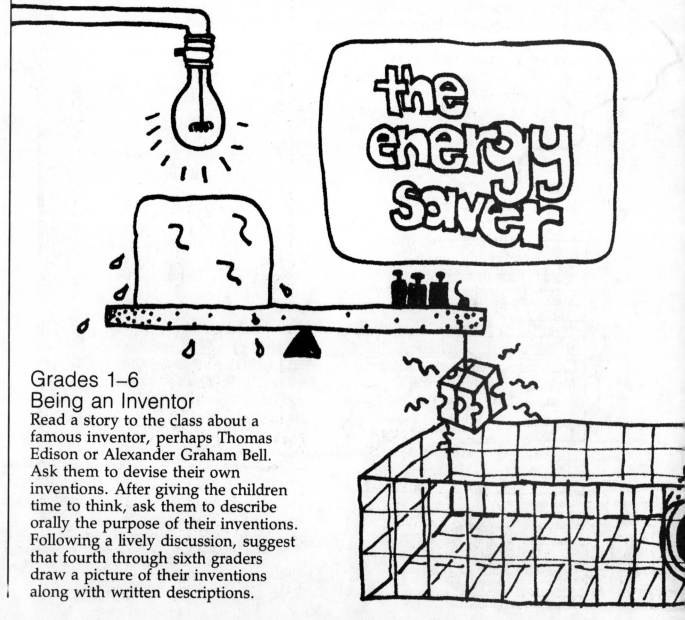

Grades 1–6
Being an Inventor

Read a story to the class about a famous inventor, perhaps Thomas Edison or Alexander Graham Bell. Ask them to devise their own inventions. After giving the children time to think, ask them to describe orally the purpose of their inventions. Following a lively discussion, suggest that fourth through sixth graders draw a picture of their inventions along with written descriptions.

Grades 3–6
Discussing Reading

Question the children about their reasons for disliking or liking reading. Ask them how to make reading more exciting. After you have recorded the ideas on the chalkboard, ask if they could carry out these ideas in their own classroom. How?

Grades 3–6
Interviewing the Principal

When the children plan their interview with the principal, have them develop their own questions. Some topics worth pursuing are his hometown, his interests as a child, his interests as an adult, his college education, his reasons for becoming a principal, some happy or sad moments, and places he has visited. The children will offer many other ideas.

Grades 3–6
Interviewing the Librarian

Before the librarian comes to class for an interview, the children should have questions ready on an experience chart or separate slips of paper. At the conclusion of the interview, the librarian can ask the children for ideas to make the library a better place to visit. Discuss which ideas to utilize in their own classroom library or in the school library.

Hi Jeff, this is Bobby talking. Last week we went on a field trip to the zoo. We got to see a baby lion that was only three weeks old. Jeff, this is Susan. We hope you can come back to school soon. I'm Jim. We did a neat science experiment today with a pendulum. I'll show you how to make one when you come back. Hi Jeff, Next week....

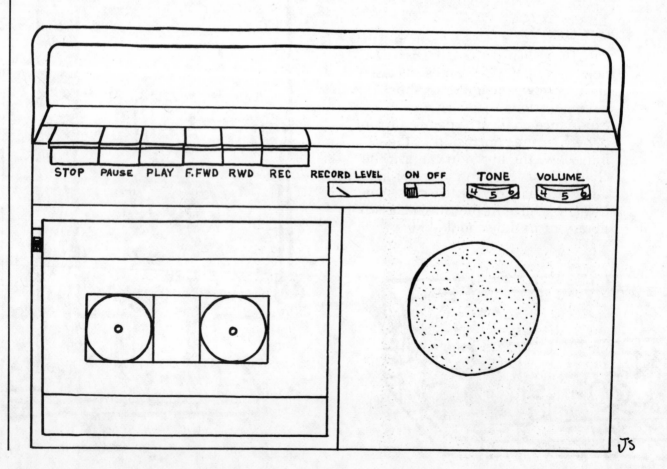

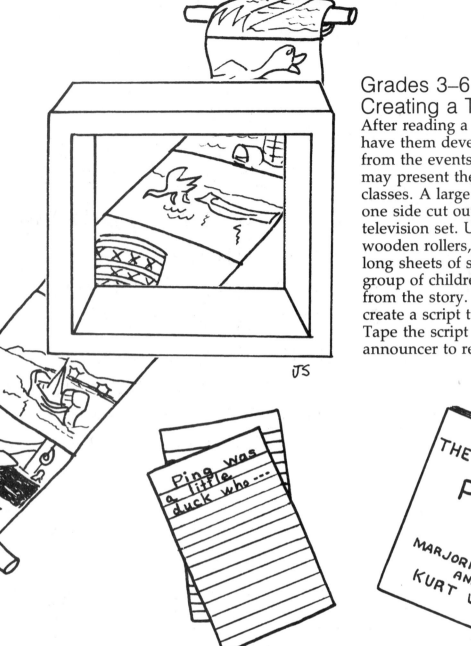

Grades 3–6
Creating a TV Show

After reading a book to the class, have them develop a television show from the events of the story. They may present the production to other classes. A large cardboard box with one side cut out will serve as a television set. Using cardboard or wooden rollers, attach and roll up long sheets of shelfpaper on which a group of children has created scenes from the story. Another group could create a script to go with the pictures. Tape the script or choose an announcer to read it "live."

Grades 1–6
Tape-recording Original Stories, Messages

Allow the children to use the tape recorder to record some of their favorite stories and poems, including original works (plays, poems, stories, and sayings). Play back the results for other classes, as well as your own. It is also fun for children to tape-record messages to a sick child who has been away from school for a week or two.

Grades 1–3
Describing Sounds Heard on a Field Trip

After having visited the zoo, the dairy, the park, the railroad station, the art museum, the library, the grocery store, the airport, or other places, ask the children to describe orally the sounds they heard and what they think made that sound. The teacher or a pupil could tape-record sounds heard on the trip and play them in the classroom.

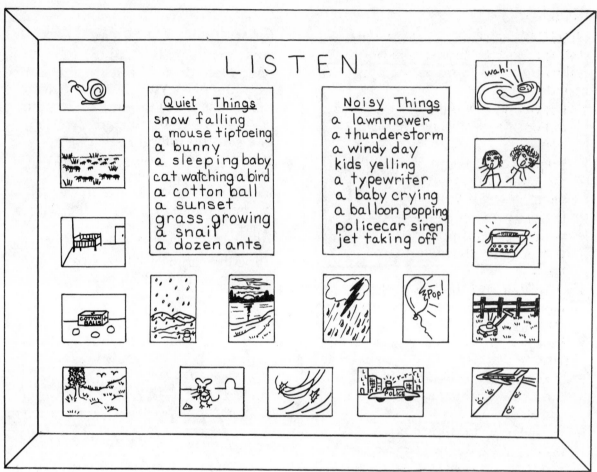

Grades 1–6
Planning a Mural

Upon returning from a field trip, ask the children to work in small groups of four or five to construct a mural about an interesting aspect of the trip. Allow the children to talk over their ideas for a mural, come to a decision, and start work. Conversations among children during planning and working stages are an important part of oral language and vocabulary development.

Grades 1–3
Making a Bulletin Board Display: Quiet/Noisy Things

Make separate experience charts about *Quiet Things* and *Noisy Things*. As the children think of all the quiet/noisy things they can, write them on the chart. Let each child choose a word or phrase from the chart to illustrate. Make a bulletin board display with the chart and the children's illustrations.

Grades 3–6
Presenting Book Reports

Ask the class to choose one of the following ways to present a book report:

1. For one or several children: create a diorama of a scene from the book.

2. Prepare a TV commercial selling the interesting points of your story, using props if you wish.

3. Dress as one of the characters in your book and pretend to be that person. Tell about your role in the book.

4. After reading the biography of a famous person, create a puppet of that individual. Use the puppet (be that person) and tell about yourself.

5. If three or four children have read the book: dramatize a scene from the story.

6. When two children have read the book: interview the author or a character, one of you being the interviewer, the other answering the questions.

7. Give an oral synopsis of the book to a small group of five children. Describe the events in sequential order.

8. Tape-record your favorite part of the story. Draw illustrations and show them to your classmates while they listen to the tape.

Grades 1–4
Making a Bulletin Board Display: Book Reports

Prepare a bulletin board display as follows: Using colored construction paper, cut out a large tree trunk with many branches growing at the top to form a tree. Write a child's name on each branch. As each child reads a book, have him orally tell you his favorite part, then write the name of the book on a precut leaf or blossom. The child should place the leaf on his branch. This project is fun to start in April because the bare tree is soon bursting with blossoms and leaves throughout the spring months.

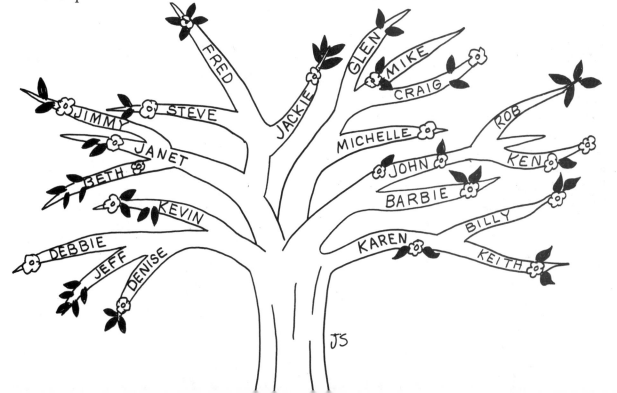

Grades 1–3
Collecting Clothes
for Dramatic Play

Keep a large box in the classroom for collecting a variety of costumes and clothes for use in dramatic play. Ask the children to bring from home such contributions as hats, gloves, purses, scarves, trousers, coats, capes, dresses, vests, shoes, various costumes, and uniforms.

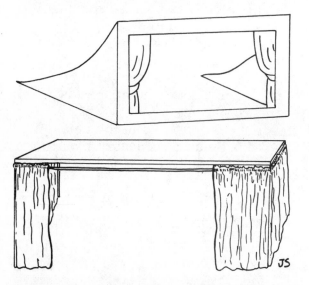

Grades 1–6
Presenting Puppet Shows

Encourage those children who wish to perform with puppets. Let them make their own puppets and stage. Two types of simple stage settings are a large box or the underside of a table, appropriately draped. Poems suited to puppet shows found in *Anthology of Children's Literature* by Johnson et al. are

- Grades 1–3 "The Duel" by Eugene Field
- Grades 3–4 "Johnathan Bing" by Beatrice Curtis Brown
- Grades 5–6 "Barbara Frietchie" by John G. Whittier

Grades 3–6
Communicating by
Pantomime

Try using pantomime with children who have not had creative dramatic experience and who feel uncomfortable in that type of situation. Play a guessing game in which each child pantomimes something and the rest of the class guesses what is happening.

1. Make some soup. Taste it. It tastes too bland. Add some seasoning.
2. Search for your sock as you get dressed in the morning. Finally, find it under the bed.
3. Search for a mitten, going from one room to another. Finally, find it in the dog's bed.
4. You smell smoke in the house. Track the smoke to its source, see what is causing it, and put out the fire.
5. Prepare lunch for yourself. Make a sandwich, open and heat a can of soup, pour a glass of milk, then peel a banana.

Grades 3–6
Pantomiming Episodes

Choose six children to participate in each of the following episodes, while the rest of the class tries to guess what is happening.

1. Pass a perfect rose from one person to another. When you receive it, examine it. Through facial expression show the class that it is a beautiful rose.
2. Pass a ball from one person to the next.
3. Pass a small rabbit from one person to the next.
4. Pass a bowl of hot soup filled to the rim.
5. Each person, one at a time, goes to a table, picks up a make-believe object, then shows by pantomime what it is by the way he handles it.

Grades 3–6
Pantomiming

Ask for volunteers to pantomime the following situations motivated by some emotion:

1. You receive a letter from your grandparents inviting you to go on a trip to California to visit Disneyland. After thinking for a few moments about all the fun you will have and how great it is for them to be able to take you, hurry into the kitchen to tell your mother the good news.
2. You walk down the street on your way home from school. Notice a three-year-old child dart into the street after a ball. You have just had time to think of the danger when a car comes rapidly around the corner toward the child. What will you do?
3. You see a third grader mistreating a small dog that you know is not his own. You become very angry, run between the boy and the dog, and rescue the frightened puppy. Then you let the boy know what you think of him.
4. You are hiking through the woods and come to a clearing. You stop suddenly, for there before you is the most beautiful sunset you have ever seen.

Grades 4–6
Pantomiming a
Classroom Situation

Ask for each of four volunteers to pantomime a situation. Hand one volunteer a card on which is written one of the following directions. The class will try to guess what is happening.

1. Come to the front of the room. Decide on a room or special place you could be. Show where you are through the physical use of objects.
2. You are to enter a room from another room. Show the class what room you have come from and the room or place you are going.
3. Enter a room. By your actions show what went on in the place you just left.
4. Enter a room. Prepare to leave the room and show by your actions what you are going to do in the other room.

Grades 1–6
Pantomiming Assigned
Actions

Choose volunteers to act out the following situations:

1. Put on an imaginary coat, hat, gloves, and boots. Take them off again and hang the coat on a hook.
2. Pick a bunch of flowers and find a thistle among them.
3. You are preparing to leave for school. You are rushed, so you quickly eat breakfast, get dressed, and brush your teeth. Just as you are going out the door the bus zooms past the house.

After the children have done the three pantomimes, have the class think of other situations and act them out, while the others guess what is happening.

Grades 1–6
Pantomiming Specific Events
Read a story to the class that contains several specific events. A good example for grades 3 through 4 is "Mr. Popper's Penguins" by Richard and Florence Atwater. Arrange for a small group of children to pantomime an incident for the rest of the class to guess. The child who guesses correctly must orally describe the event, with support from other class members for any missing details. Choose other children to act out the other incidents.

Grades 1–2
Pantomiming Special Stories
Many children's stories and poems are especially suited to acting out by young children. They can pantomime these stories and actions either while the teacher is in the process of reading the story or following the reading. The following story titles are appropriate for this activity:
- "Little Princess Goodnight" by Bill Martin
- "The Lorax" by Dr. Seuss
- "There's a Nightmare in My Closet" by Mercer Mayer
- "The Silent Concert" by Mary Leister
- Mother Goose rhymes:
     "The Three Little Kittens"
     "Little Miss Muffet"
     "Humpty Dumpty"
     "Old Mother Hubbard"

Grades 1–6
Pantomiming Vacation Happenings
Ask the children to think of something they saw on a recent vacation. Allow each child to pantomime what happened, while the rest of the class tries to guess what he saw.

Grades 1–6
Pantomiming for the Whole Class
The whole class can participate in the following situations at their seats, near their desks, or sitting and standing in a circle. As the teacher describes the action each class member should

1. hike up a rocky hill, tiptoe down the hallway, walk on an icy sidewalk, walk down a muddy path, walk in a pair of sandals that are too big
2. sew and stick himself with a needle
3. pick up a baby
4. try to find his slippers and robe in the dark bedroom
5. drink cocoa that is too hot
6. bite into a sour apple
7. smell something unpleasant and try to decide what it is
8. see a building on fire
9. see and smell a new bloom on the rosebush
10. see the new bike his dad just bought for him

Grades 1–2
Role-playing a Kite

Recruit someone to be a kite stuck in a tree. A gust of wind comes along to release it. The kite describes how it feels and what it sees as it is flying.

Grades 1–6
Role-playing
a New Student

Ask the children to role-play the situation of a new student in class. The next day ask the children to be themselves and think of ways to make a new student feel welcome in class. Have them role-play their ideas.

Grades 1–2
Role-playing
a Caterpillar

Request a volunteer to role-play a caterpillar eating leaves, spinning its cocoon, resting, then emerging as a lovely butterfly.

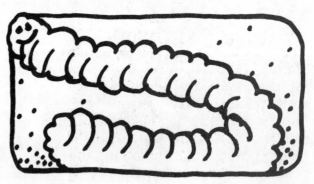

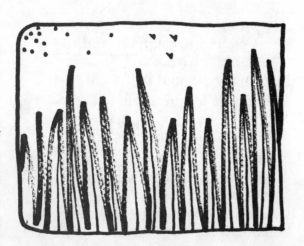

Grades 1–2
Role-playing a
Blade of Grass

Invite a child to role-play the following situation: Imagine that you are a blade of grass. You are soaking wet from spring rains. Summer comes and you are so thirsty that you are turning brown. A summer shower freshens you again. Now you are growing tall. Watch out, the lawn mower is coming!

Grades 1–2
Role-playing a Rabbit
and a Turtle

Introduce the following situation for two children to dramatize: You are a baby rabbit who has lost its mother and cannot find its way home. You come upon a turtle slowly moving along and ask for help. How does he help you find your way home?

Grades 1–2
Role-playing
before a Mirror

Display a full-length mirror in the room where the children will have an opportunity to see themselves. They can role-play parts of their choice in front of the mirror. Perhaps the teacher could read the story "Caps for Sale" by Esphur Slobodkina to the class. After the children have talked about the story, ask them to bring a variety of hats to school. In a few days, when several hats such as a baseball cap, a lady's hat full of feathers, a bus driver's hat, a serviceman's hat, a baker's hat, and others have been collected, let the children try on the hats, using the mirror to role-play by themselves or with another child. Have a few children talk about the responsibilities of the person wearing the hat.

Grades 1–3
Role-playing by Phone

Provide the opportunity for children to use a play telephone to dramatize dialogue. Encourage conversations such as:

1. Mother talking to the doctor about her sick child
2. Dad calling the airport for plane reservations
3. a child calling his best friend to tell him about breaking a leg while skiing
4. Grandma calling a friend just to gossip
5. a child talking to Dad at the office about the fire drill that turned out to be real
6. a child talking to Grandma about the nicest thing that happened at school that day
7. Mother calling the fire department to report a fire
8. a policeman talking to the mother of a lost child

Grades 1–2
Role-playing Pets

Display pictures of pets on the bulletin board. Ask the children to choose a pet, then have two children act out a puppy meeting a cat for the first time; a mother cat teaching her kitten how to take a bath (this will probably be a tongue-licking exercise); a parakeet flying outside its cage, spotted by the cat; a pony who must say goodbye to his mother because he has a new owner.

Grades 1–3
Caring for a Pet

Read the story "Part-time Dog" by Jane Thayer to the class. Talk about what happened to Brownie, the stray dog. Ask, "What other things could have happened to Brownie or any stray dog?" Discuss the responsibility of caring for a pet and the reasons for dog tags, shots, and leash laws. The class might like to dramatize Brownie's story or a stray dog story of their own making.

Grades 1–3
Creating Dialogue

Ask for volunteers to participate in a situation in which two children create their own dialogue to resolve the given situation. Such situations might include:

1. Your parents have just given you a puppy for your birthday. Carry it over to your best friend's house and tell him all about it.
2. Tell your father about the five-dollar bill you found on your way to the store.
3. You have found a toy poodle who needs a home, but your mother says you can't have another dog. Try to persuade her to keep it.
4. You wanted some skis for Christmas but when you opened the present from your parents, it was a new wallet containing twenty-five dollars instead.
5. You and your mother are planning a birthday party for you. What are your plans?

Grades 1–6
Stimulating Imagination

Display pictures of such objects as a musical instrument, a toy, some new clothes, a car, and some garden tools. Ask for volunteers to role-play an object in one of the pictures. Explain that the child will be the object and must tell about an event that occurred at some time in the object's life. The object should express its feelings about what happened. Continue until all the pictures have been dramatized.

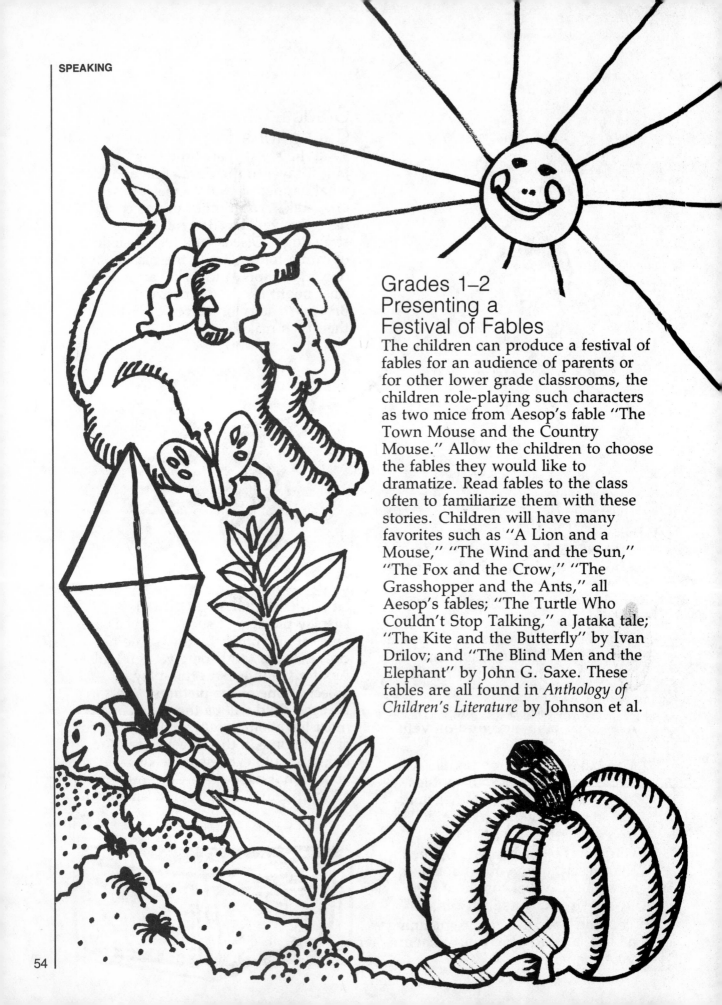

Grades 1–2
Presenting a
Festival of Fables

The children can produce a festival of fables for an audience of parents or for other lower grade classrooms, the children role-playing such characters as two mice from Aesop's fable "The Town Mouse and the Country Mouse." Allow the children to choose the fables they would like to dramatize. Read fables to the class often to familiarize them with these stories. Children will have many favorites such as "A Lion and a Mouse," "The Wind and the Sun," "The Fox and the Crow," "The Grasshopper and the Ants," all Aesop's fables; "The Turtle Who Couldn't Stop Talking," a Jataka tale; "The Kite and the Butterfly" by Ivan Drilov; and "The Blind Men and the Elephant" by John G. Saxe. These fables are all found in *Anthology of Children's Literature* by Johnson et al.

Grades 1–4
Creating New Drama
from Old Stories

Set up some "Just Imagine" happenings based upon favorite stories with which the children are already well acquainted. Have the children act out what happens in the following situations:

Grades 1-3

1. Hansel wakes up in the woods and finds Gretel gone. How does he feel? Where was Gretel? What does Hansel do?

2. Little Red Riding Hood meets a spaceman in the forest on the way to Grandmother's house. What does she do?

3. Cinderella does not hear the clock strike twelve at the ball. Why doesn't she hear the clock? Does her fairy godmother do anything?

4. Jack does not plant the bean. What happens to Jack and his mother? What happens to the bean? Do Jack and his mother remain poor?

Grades 3-4

1. Aladdin gives his wonderful lamp to a poor old man who needs warmth and light. What does the old man say to Aladdin? What does he do with the lamp? What finally happens?

2. Pinocchio tells a lie. His nose does not grow longer, but something else happens to him. What happens when Pinocchio tells a lie? What lie does he tell? What finally happens to Pinocchio?

3. Snow White discovers a little tailor's house instead of the seven dwarves' house. How does the tailor help Snow White? Is the tailor the queen's friend? How does the prince find Snow White?

Grades 1–2
Dramatizing Stories

Stories that lend themselves to dramatization are:

- "Little Tim and the Brave Sea Captain" by E. Ardizzone
- "Chanticleer and the Fox" by Geoffrey Chaucer
- "In the Forest" by Marie Hall Ets
- "The Happy Lion" by Louise Fatio

Read each story to the class. Let the class decide where the story takes place, how many and who the characters will be, and what they are going to do. Each character can decide what he wants to say as the story progresses; let the children decide how they want to handle the story.

THE MONSTER THAT ATE THE WORLD

A PLAY BY MR. HARRISON'S FIFTH GRADE CLASS

Grades 1–6
Creating Plays

A teacher and the class can develop and create their own plays. Motivating the class to volunteer ideas for a play is easily accomplished by posing a variety of questions. As the children share their ideas, record them on the chalkboard. Fill in a simple outline already written there, stating type of story, setting of the action, characters and their personal qualities, and events or situations that occur.

To begin, ask them about their favorite types of stories, perhaps real-life, animal, mystery, humorous, and so on. They will have to come to a general consensus about the type of story they want to produce. Other questions for a teacher to ask are: Where will the events of this story take place? How many characters shall we have and what shall we name them? What are their personal qualities? What should the characters do in the story? What events, including predicaments and circumstances, would you like to create?

Decide upon a beginning scene and work your way through the story with general scenes and their sequence. Ask the children who would like to participate in the play and which character they would like to become. Develop each scene utilizing spontaneous dialogue. Have fun!

BIBLIOGRAPHY:
Part Two

Ardizzone, Edward. *Little Tim and the Brave Sea Captain.* New York: Henry Z. Walck, Inc., 1955.

Atwater, Richard and Florence. *Mr. Popper's Penguins.* Boston: Little, Brown, & Company, 1938.

Calhoun, Mary. *The Witch of Hissing Hill.* New York: William Morrow & Company, 1964.

Chaucer, Geoffrey. *Chanticleer and the Fox.* New York: Thomas Y. Crowell, 1958.

Ets, Marie Hall. *In the Forest.* New York: Viking Press Inc., 1970.

Fatio, Louise. *The Happy Lion.* New York: McGraw-Hill Book Company, Inc., 1954.

Fleischman, Sid. *Longbeard the Wizard.* Boston: Little, Brown, & Company, 1970.

Johnson, Edna; Scott, Carrie E.; and Sickels, Evelyn R. *Anthology of Children's Literature.* Boston: Houghton Mifflin Company, 1970.
Poems–"The Duel," Eugene Field
        "Jonathan Bing," Beatrice
        Curtis Brown
        "Barbara Frietchie," John
        Greenleaf Whittier
        Mother Goose Rhymes
Aesop's Fables–"The Town Mouse and
        the Country Mouse"
        "A Lion and a Mouse"
        "The Wind and the Sun"
        "The Fox and the Crow"
        "The Grasshopper and the
        Ants"
Jataka Tale–"The Turtle Who Couldn't
        Stop Talking"
Fables–"The Kite and the Butterfly,"
        Ivan Drilov
        "The Blind Men and the
        Elephant," John G. Saxe

Leister, Mary. *The Silent Concert.* Indianapolis: Bobbs-Merrill, 1970.

Martin, Bill, Jr. *Little Princess Goodnight.* New York: Kinder-Owl Books: Literature Series, Holt, Rinehart, & Winston, Inc., 1971.

Mayer, Mercer. *There's a Nightmare in My Closet.* New York: Dial Press, 1968.

Seuss, Dr. *The Lorax.* New York: Random House, Inc., 1971.

Slobodkina, Esphur. *Caps for Sale.* Reading, Mass.: Young Scott Books, Addison-Wesley Publishing Company, Inc., 1947.

Steig, William. *Sylvester and the Magic Pebble.* New York: Simon & Schuster, Inc., 1969.

Stephenson, Dorothy. *How to Scare a Lion.* Chicago: Follett Publishing Company, 1965.

Thayer, Jane. *Part-Time Dog.* New York: William Morrow & Company, 1954.

—————. *What's a Ghost Going to Do?* New York: William Morrow & Company, 1966.

Ward, Lynd. *The Silver Pony.* Boston: Houghton Mifflin Company, 1973.

EXPANDING VOCABULARY

My Foods Dictionary

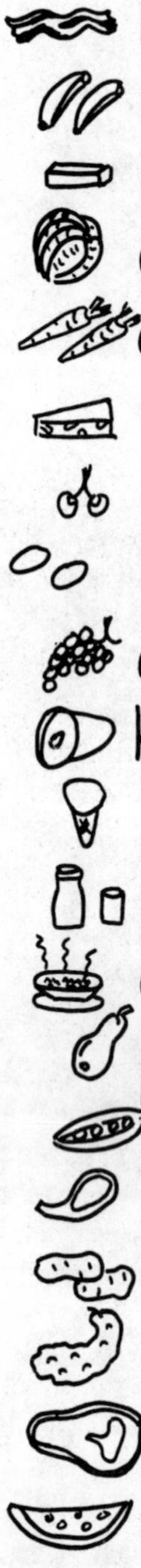

bacon - meat

bananas - fruit

butter - a dairy product

cantalope - fruit

carrots - vegetable

cheese - a dairy product

cherries - fruit

eggs - a dairy product

grapes - fruit

ham - meat

ice cream - a dairy product

milk - a dairy product

oatmeal - cereal

pears - fruit

peas - vegetable

pork chops - meat

potatoes - vegetable

squash - vegetable

steak - meat

watermelon - fruit

Grades 3–6
Making an Illustrated
Word Dictionary

Ask the children to collect vocabulary words relating to a hobby (pets, music, painting, coin collecting) or special project, and define and alphabetize each word in the form of a dictionary. To add interest, illustrate these word dictionaries. The class can make many other types of dictionaries during the year about such topics as kinds of boats, buildings, and bridges; modes of transportation; and various leisure-time activities.

Sixth graders might attempt an illustrated dictionary of famous people. Have them use personalities they have read about in their social studies, science, and reading units. Perhaps a few children will be interested in using a well-known figure in biographies they have read from the library. This type of activity works best as a large-group activity utilizing committees.

Grades 2–4
Pantomiming Descriptive
Words

Using an opaque projector, display pictures of animals or people that describe adjectives such as delighted, amazed, angry, happy, guilty, grim, questioning, impatient, and excited. Discuss each word as the children study its matching picture. Allow the class to pantomime the expressions they see in each picture.

Grades 1–6
Developing a
Vocabulary Booklet

Have each child develop a vocabulary booklet to use during the year. The child will record any word that is new or unusual and use it in a simple sentence in order to derive the correct meaning. The teacher should help the child with any hard-to-spell word. The children can copy many of the words from experience charts or lists compiled by the teacher after the class has read a story, worked on a special science or social studies unit, or developed a class story. Allow the children to help each other create sentences to accompany each new word. Have them illustrate some of the words.

Grades 3–6
Having a Treasure
Hunt for New Words

Have a treasure hunt for new, unusual, and interesting words or phrases while the children are reading self-chosen material from the library or home. Ask them to record the words in their vocabulary notebooks. Set aside a time for the children to share their word lists with the class. Presentation of the word lists can take many forms: a poster, sentences written on story paper, pictures of the words, a story utilizing all the words in the child's list, a tape recording, a bulletin board display, a picture dictionary, or a word dictionary. Display these projects for others to study.

Grades 1–4
Describing Name Words

After reading a book or story to the class, ask the children to name some things in the story. Record six or seven names on the chalkboard. A list such as the following is possible: tent, crowd, popcorn, dog, clown, wind. Ask the children to think of some interesting, imaginative words that describe each thing on the list.

Grades 1–6
Charting New Vocabulary Words

List on a chart or story paper all special vocabulary words discovered in a unit of study. Illustrate as many words as possible right on the chart. First and second graders can find pictures of the words in magazines and place them next to the words. The children can readily refer to the chart for spelling purposes as well as for choosing a good, usable vocabulary word for their creative writing and reports.

airy	roomy	circus	tent
noisy	restless	laughing	crowd
delicious	salty	buttery	popcorn
___	___	___	dog
___	___	___	clown
___	___	___	wind

Grades 3–6
Using Descriptive
Words from Movies

After watching movies such as "The Waterfalls," "The Geyser," or "Pigs," ask the class to think of words describing the waterfall, the geyser, and the pigs as seen in the respective movies. Display the list of words recorded on chart paper. The children can refer to the list later for a creative writing activity (see Using Films, page 110).

Grades 2–6
Seeing Words within Words

Training the eye to see smaller words within a larger word develops verbal versatility. List a column of fairly long words on the chalkboard and direct the children to write down all the smaller words they find within the words on the board. Sample words are strapping (strap, trap, rap, ping, in), glowing (glow, low, wing, win, owing, in), and stroller (stroll, troll, roll, roller).

Variation: Using all the letters in a word, form as many words as possible. An example is glowing (owl, log, wig, gown, now, won, and gang). Explain that jumbled words are anagrams.

THE GEYSER

veils of mist
shower of water
showery spray
bubbling kettle
mysterious puddle
simmery surge
sinister swell
lively spurt
shooting streams
spouting
gushing wetness

JS

PIGS

squirming
filthy
dirty
wiggly
delighted
heavy
curly-cue tails
oozing mud
massive bodies

JS

Grades 1–4
Making Food
Picture Folders

Discuss some foods that each child's family has on the picnic table at a cookout. Record these words on lists in categories such as meats, fruits, vegetables, drinks, desserts, dairy foods, and breads. Children can make individual folders containing sheets of construction paper, category titles, correct food names, and illustrations or pictures cut out from magazines. Small groups of children can make posters indicating the titles, food names, and illustrations.

Foods at a Cookout
cole slaw
potato salad
baked beans
hamburgers
hot dogs, buns
apples grapes
carrot strips
steak
chicken
iced tea
brownies

FOODS COOKOUT

Meat
Hamburger
Hot Dogs
Steak
Chicken
Spareribs

Apples
Grapes
Bananas

Grades 1–6
Displaying Pictures

Display on the bulletin board some interesting pictures that show something happening, such as children playing in the ocean, a child eating an apple, a family picnic, or a child with a sad expression. Ask such questions as: "How does the child feel?" Possible answers are: sad, scared, anxious, afraid, or hurt. "How does the apple taste?" Possible answers are: delicious, juicy, sweet, tasty, or tart.

As an individualized activity for fourth, fifth, and sixth graders, mount the pictures on colored construction paper and write a question at the top of each picture. Place these in a folder. The child can record answers on a piece of notebook paper. Later hold an individual conference or class discussion about the choice of words.

Grades 3–6
Using the Author's Descriptive Words

While reading a story to the class, or after a story is finished, talk together about the descriptive words the author uses. Try to use some of them during the day. Have the children place the words in their vocabulary booklets and on the room chart or ask the class members to use these words in written sentences of their own.

Grades 3–5
Illustrating Food Composition

Draw a single food item such as a casserole or a cake. Underneath the picture, break down this item into its ingredients. Research the source of each ingredient, and, on a third line at the bottom of the chart, draw or find a picture of the ingredient's source. A sample chart follows.

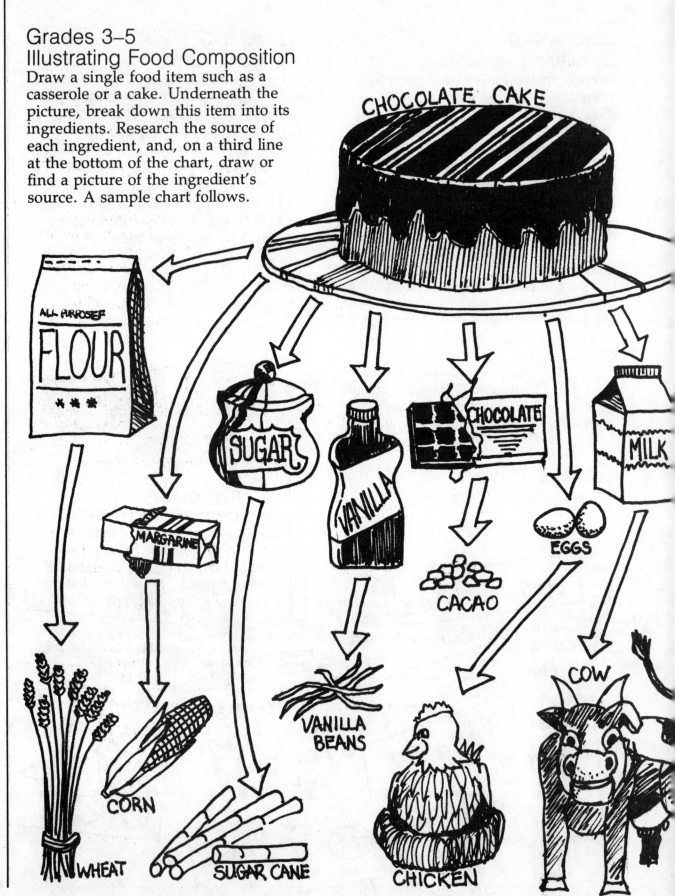

Grades 2–4
Building a Word Chart

A teacher can initiate building a word chart by using an overhead projector and focusing the children's attention upon a word. Ask the children to offer as many words as they can with the projected word in it. A sample list follows, using the word snow.

snowshoe   snowsuit   snowstorm
snowflake   snowplow   snowy
snowman   snowfall   snowdrift

Other words to use for building a word chart are school, fire, house, life, and light.

For use with a small group of children, write the compound word snowman on the board. Draw three circles representing a snowman above the word. For each compound word using snow_____, each child places eyes, nose, mouth, pipe, hat, scarf, arms, and buttons on the snowman. List each given word under the word snowman.

For a similar activity, draw one color of a curving rainbow on a large piece of manila drawing paper. Write the compound word rainbow under the drawing. For each compound word with rain_____ in it, a child draws another color on the rainbow.

Grades 2–4
Describing Objects

Ask each child to cut out a picture of any object from a magazine, stapling or gluing it to the upper portion of a piece of notebook paper. Record words given by the children describing the looks, feel, and taste or smell of the different kinds of objects, as well as describing what the objects can do. Discuss the words, then ask the children to write about *their* object in paragraph form. They should use some of the words on the chalkboard in their sentences. The written list on the chalkboard may look something like the following:

Object	How does it look?	How does it taste or smell?	How does it feel?	What can it do?
dog	long-haired happy frisky anxious	clean sour sweaty	shaggy soft hairy	chase beg whine bark pant growl
ice cream cone	delicious tempting round like snow cone-shaped	creamy nutty vanilla	smooth crunchy wet cold	melt plop disappear drip

Grades 4–6
Choosing Synonyms

Discuss with the children a variety of words to use in writing a paragraph about a squirrel: it, he or him, she or her, that agile creature, small bushy-tailed animal, etc. In place of the name Sally, substitute other words: she, her, my sister, a three-year-old scamp, petite miss, sassy tomboy, a brave girl. After discussing several examples, have the boys and girls pick a strip of paper from a shoebox on which is written the name of a famous person, an animal, or the name of a relative (grandmother, father, brother). Then ask each child to think of several words to use in place of the name. Suggest constructing a paragraph using the words chosen.

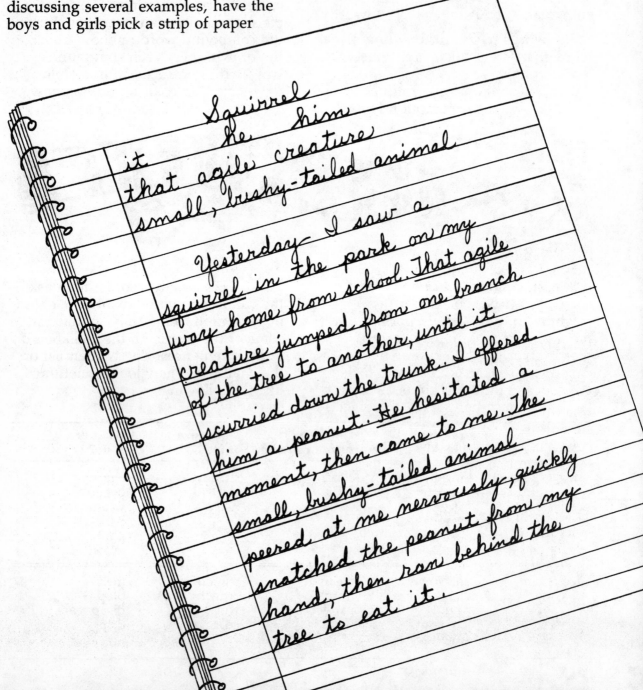

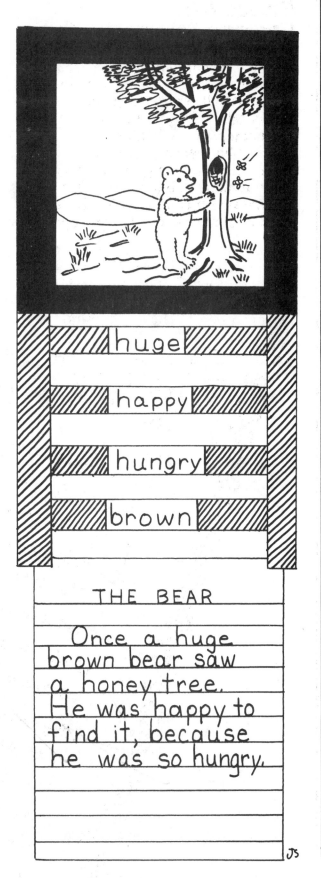

Grades 3–6
Making a Picture-word Ladder

In order to make a picture-word ladder, ask the children to cut colorful pictures of any object or living thing from a magazine and back them with pieces of colored construction paper. Attach word cards describing the picture below the picture with strips of construction paper. If you wish, use another picture with descriptive words on the opposite side. Extra words can be added at any time. Following this activity, the children may want to use one of the picture-word ladders to create a descriptive paragraph about the picture, using some or all of the words on the ladder. Attach the story to the bottom of the ladder. These picture-word ladders can be hung by string and used as mobiles in the classroom.

Grades 4–6
Studying Compound Words

Separate compound words into their components. Is the meaning of a compound word always equal to the sum of its parts? Find some compound words that make sense if broken down and some that seem ludicrous if their parts are considered separately. Examples: handwriting, greenhouse, beeswax, seaweed, newspaper, handyman, strawberry, raspberry, lighthouse, oatmeal, eyebrows, doorway, broomstick, playground, shoestring, notebook, downstairs, goldfish, moonlight, seacoast, cowboy, birthday, inside, highway, bookcase, grasshopper, driveway, headlight, understand.

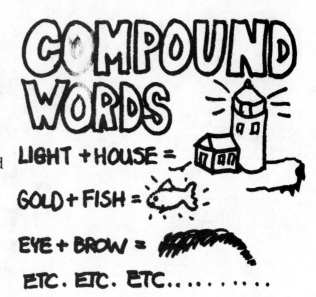

COMPOUND WORDS

LIGHT + HOUSE =

GOLD + FISH =

EYE + BROW =

ETC. ETC. ETC.........

TELEscope

Grades 4–6
Examining Related Words

Related words often help children develop meanings for words. With a teacher's help, a list and discussion of the following words aid in determining word meaning: *tele*graph, *tele*pathy, *tele*phone, *tele*scope, *tele*vision, *tele*thon. After examining these words the class will be able to determine that *tele* often means "far." Another group of words can be used in a similar manner: *auto*biography, *auto*graph, *auto*mat, *auto*matic; *auto* meaning "self, oneself, or itself."

Grades 1–6
Using Human Interest Pictures

Show the class an interesting, unusual, or stimulating picture on the opaque projector. Some excellent pictures to use with this type of activity can be found in the daily newspaper, where human interest photographs are plentiful. A picture of a bridge that collapsed or a picture of a truck, too high for an underpass that sheared off its top, would be good examples. One might see a photograph of a monkey drinking from a water fountain or a car sitting on the front entry of a school. Ask questions such as: "How could this have been avoided?" "What do you think happened?" "Who made this happen?" "Who do you think was responsible for this?" Ask the children to describe certain aspects of the picture using pertinent descriptive words. For example, after the children have viewed a picture of the monkey, ask for words describing how the water felt to the monkey as he drank it. Ask how people reacted upon seeing such a sight.

What might have caused this
bridge to collapse?

Let's think of some words to
describe the bridge.

If there were cars on the
bridge, how did the people
feel as they started to fall?

How were the survivors rescued?

Tell your version of the catastrophe.

Grades 3–5
Creating New Animal Names

Have the class make up new animal names by combining two names, and make up a story with the new animal as a hero or a villain. Children might create such animal names as the following: beavermine, buffalope, ocelotter, cattler, kangarooster, elephanteater. Illustrate each story.

Grades 3–6
Making Story Fillers for Halloween and Other Occasions

Children thrive on this kind of activity. First, find or write a short story and remove all the descriptive words. Ask the children to think of a good, imaginative word describing a noun and write it on a piece of paper. As the teacher reads the story aloud from the chalkboard or a large sheet of story paper, each child in turn should contribute his own word at each pause. The teacher or a child inserts the word into the empty space. The results sometimes sound sensible but often are pure nonsense.

A teacher can create stories for special occasions such as the first snow, Halloween, Thanksgiving,

Christmas, a windy day, and others. A story created at Halloween time follows.

In the middle of the _____, _____ night Jimmy heard a _____ sound. It frightened him so much that he ran into his brother's _____ room to tell him about it. While they were talking, they both heard something that sounded like a _____, _____ witch cackling to someone in the _____, _____ garage. Together they tiptoed down the _____ stairs to investigate. As Jimmy placed his _____ hand on the _____ knob of the _____ door, a _____ scream tortured the boys' _____ ears. Shaking and stumbling into the _____ garage, the _____ boys were startled to see a pair of _____ eyes staring at them. Quickly switching on the _____ lights, the boys saw a _____, _____ cat standing on top of the _____ car. His _____ back was humped and his _____ tail pointed upward. When Jimmy and his brother realized it was only a _____ cat, they laughed and laughed.

Using the same story, ask each child to supply orally a sensible descriptive word at the pauses.

Give fifth or sixth graders, working in pairs, the opportunity to create their own story fillers for the class if they wish.

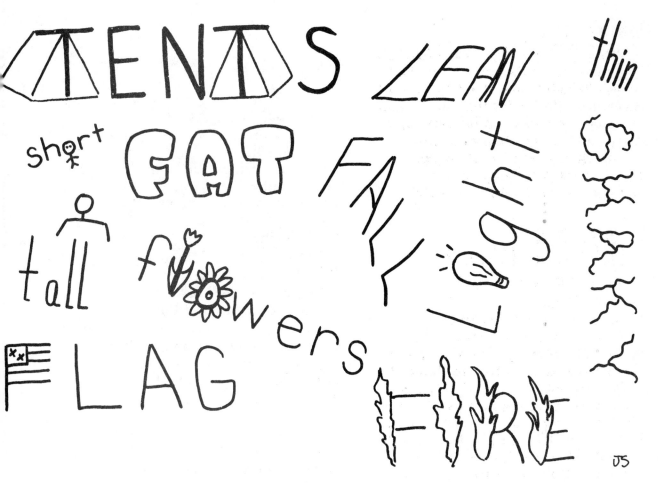

Grades 3–6
Picturing Words

A unique and enjoyable activity that
appeals to children and teaches the
genuine meaning of words is word
drawing. *Short* would be drawn with
short letters next to the word *tall*,
whose letters extend very high. The
word *fat* might be drawn with
extended, roly-poly letters. The word
penny might be colored copper and
drawn in a circular manner. Other
possibilities are the words *lean* drawn
at an extreme slant, *flag* drawn with a
flag in place of the *f*, and *balloon*
drawn with strings attached to the *o*'s.
Give the children a few models such
as the words mentioned above and
they will create many, many more of
their own. They could work either
individually or in small groups,
making picture vocabulary posters,
charts, paragraphs, or stories.

Grades 3–6
Collecting Special Words

A teacher can easily motivate an
interest in words. Each day, add a
special word to your ladder of words
attached to the wall. The children
may add words to those the teacher
provides. Start with the word *mystical*.
Discuss its root and meaning, then
ask for a few oral sentences using the
new word. Choose a child to place
the first word step on the ladder. The
words the teacher chooses should not
be too difficult for the class to
pronounce or understand. Tell the
children to utilize their dictionaries.
Other special words for sixth-grade
children are ghastly, century,
millennium, exasperation,
seismograph, tureen, whimsical,
flabbergasted, beckon, dowdy, and
hummock.

Grades 3–6
Reversing the Letters
of Words

Another way for a teacher to create an interest in words for the children in class is by giving them three words such as *tot, eye,* and *nun.* Ask, "What are the similarities within these words?" Then ask them to think of other words that could be reversed and still remain the same. Record them on the chalkboard. Ask one of the children to create a poster for the room using all the words.

Another poster could be made of words that, when reversed, will become entirely new words such as *mood* and *doom*.

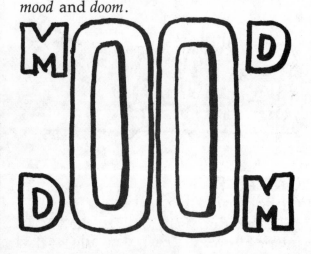

Grades 1–6
Recording Action Words
on Shelfpaper

Attach a long piece of shelfpaper on the tack rail or wall and let it hang to the floor. Across the top write the title *Action Words.* Ask the children to write action words they have observed in school during the day. Some examples are skid (gym shoes), soar (on the swing), squint (in the sun), and whisper (in class). Children can add action words to this list each day.

Grades 5–6
Using Maps
for a Treasure Hunt

A treasure hunt for names of cities, countries, states, etc. is fun for children as well as educational. Divide the class into six separate groups. Each group will be given appropriate maps and two or three examples to help start their hunt.

Ask group A to find the names of presidents that are also names of United States cities, for example, Monroe, Michigan and Lincoln, Nebraska.

Ask group B to find names of famous people that are also names of United States cities, for example, Franklin, New Hampshire and Lafayette, Indiana.

Ask group C to find cities in the United States also found in other countries, for example, Rome, New York (Italy) and Toledo, Ohio (Spain).

Ask group D to find the names of other countries that are also city names found in the United States, for example, Peru, Indiana and Cuba, New York.

Ask group E to find names of national parks that have the names of natural features, for examples, Grand Canyon and Mammoth Cave.

Ask group F to find the names of natural features found in the United States (national park names not allowed) that are city names, for example, Mesa, Arizona; Long Island, New York; and Apple Valley, California.

Allow each group to present their findings in a variety of ways. Perhaps they will decide to make a poster or chart, draw or develop a salt and flour map, or create a song, poem, or story.

Grades 4–6
Adding Words
Instead of adding up numbers, add up words. Examples:

ominous clouds
+cooling temperatures
———————————
a rainshower

high speed·
+reckless driving
———————————
a traffic accident

zesty cheese
+tangy tomatoes
———————————
tempting pizza

hanging icycles
+soaring temperatures
———————————
dripping water

Grades 3–6
Collecting Action Words
Suggest that a group of children go to the chalkboard and write an exciting action word in place of a verb in the sentence "The horse ran across the field." Several words to replace *ran* are *galloped, trotted, raced,* and *streaked.* Select a child to record these words on the class list titled *Action Words.* Try another sentence such as "Jody *ran* all the way to the store." Children might offer the words *dashed, rushed, skipped, hustled,* and *hurried.* Next use the verb *move* in several sentences. The group might collect such possibilities as *crawled, bounced, flew, flitted, slid, ambled, tiptoed, bounded, slithered,* and *climbed.*

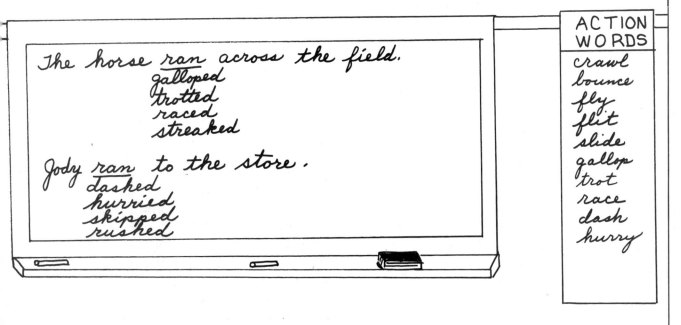

JS

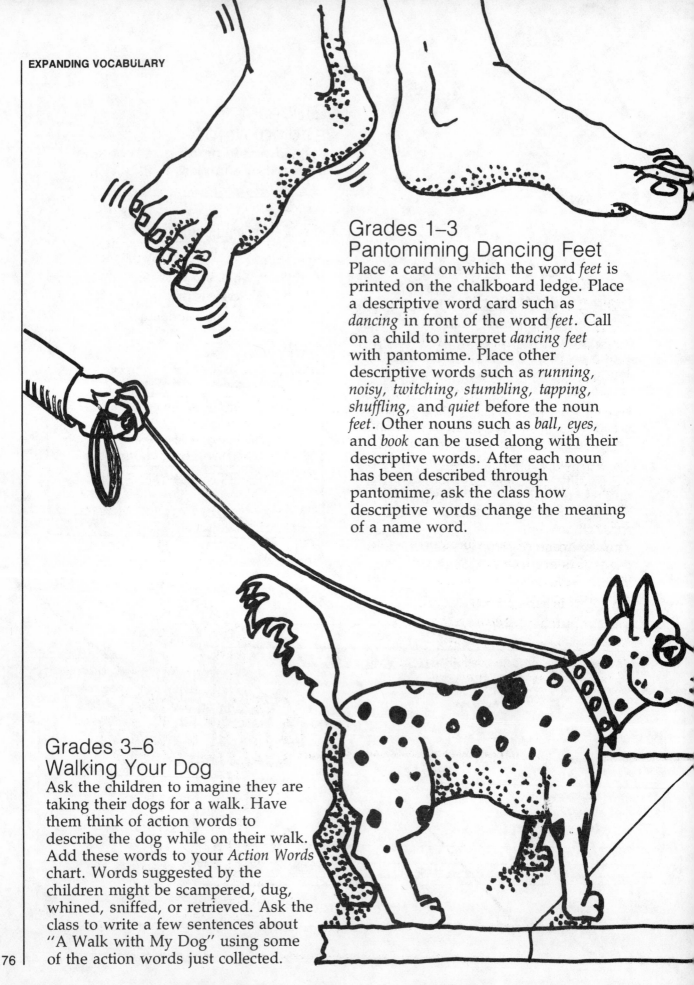

Grades 1–3
Pantomiming Dancing Feet

Place a card on which the word *feet* is printed on the chalkboard ledge. Place a descriptive word card such as *dancing* in front of the word *feet*. Call on a child to interpret *dancing feet* with pantomime. Place other descriptive words such as *running*, *noisy*, *twitching*, *stumbling*, *tapping*, *shuffling*, and *quiet* before the noun *feet*. Other nouns such as *ball, eyes*, and *book* can be used along with their descriptive words. After each noun has been described through pantomime, ask the class how descriptive words change the meaning of a name word.

Grades 3–6
Walking Your Dog

Ask the children to imagine they are taking their dogs for a walk. Have them think of action words to describe the dog while on their walk. Add these words to your *Action Words* chart. Words suggested by the children might be scampered, dug, whined, sniffed, or retrieved. Ask the class to write a few sentences about "A Walk with My Dog" using some of the action words just collected.

Grades 1–4
Using Pictures of
Pets or People

Arrange a bulletin board of pictures of pets or people who are active. Ask the class to think of some action words needed to describe the action in each picture, or ask the children what they see happening in the pictures. Answers might include:

I see a monkey *climbing* a ladder.

I see a swan *swimming* in a pond.

A snake is *slithering* among the branches.

In the case of people pictures these sentences are likely:

A man is *carrying* a suitcase.

That girl is *eating* a sandwich.

I see a butcher *wrapping* some meat.

The children can develop a list of these action words and add it to the class list posted on the wall.

Grades 4–6
Displaying Word Collections

Allow the class or a small group to develop their own bulletin board display from the new vocabulary words collected during a health, science, or social studies unit calling for specialized vocabulary. Their words and definitions could be colorfully and descriptively illustrated, keyed, or diagramed.

Grades 1–6
Learning Word
Meaning from Context

On the chalkboard, list words that are probably unfamiliar to the class and are taken from a variety of materials. Ask the children to listen carefully and see if they can discover the words' meanings from the context of the material read to them. Material from a newspaper article, a magazine story, or a passage from a book is appropriate. Tape-record the material and use it as an individualized lesson.

Grades 2–3
Building a Sentence

Across the chalkboard write the headings *What Happened, Where, When,* and *Descriptive Word.* To the left and above the headings write a short, simple sentence such as "We saw a peacock." Ask a child to rewrite the sentence telling *what happened.* The next child will write *where* it happened, followed by someone who specifies *when* it happened. The last person rewrites the whole sentence and adds a word to *describe* the peacock. The final sentence may look something like this: "Yesterday at the zoo, we saw a beautiful peacock spread its tail." Try working several sentences in a similar manner.

I heard the baby.

Beth saw a clown.

Kevin felt a raindrop.

Dad saw the spaceship.

Grades 1–2
"Who Is Sad?"

The teacher can begin by thinking of a word such as *sad.* Then say, "Hello, Mrs. *Sad*ington, who is *sad*?" Any girl who can think of a rhyming word answers, "The lad," or perhaps, "Dad." The replies can be sensible or just plain nonsense, as long as the word rhymes. Next the teacher can look around at the boys and say, "Hello, Mr. *Funny*bones, who is *funny*?" A reply might be, "Bunny." A child might try the next one by saying, "Hello, Mrs. *Wet*more, who is *wet*?" A possible answer is, "My pet," or, "A jet." The teacher or the children will invent many more. The opportunity to think of a person's name (Mrs. Wetmore) to accompany the word that he chooses to be rhymed (wet) fosters creativity within the child.

We saw a peacock.

What Happened

We saw a peacock <u>spread its tail</u>.

Where

We saw a peacock spread its tail <u>at the zoo</u>.

When

We saw a peacock spread its tail at the zoo <u>yesterday</u>.

Descriptive Word

We saw a <u>beautiful</u> peacock spread its tail at the zoo yesterday.

JS

Grades 1–6
Using Covered Pictures

Using a large bulletin board, create an art gallery. Choose several interesting colored pictures from magazines, attaching them at or below the children's eye level. Cover each picture with a colorful piece of construction paper out of which a small rectangle has been cut. Only a segment of the picture will appear. Above the pictures, provide the caption *Can you guess what is in the picture?* Direct the children to lift the paper frame after they have made a guess.

Tell the children (in grades 4 through 6) to write a descriptive sentence on a piece of notebook paper about two or three of the numbered pictures. Ask each child to exchange papers with another person and try to decide which picture is being described.

Grade 6
Making a Bulletin Board on Prefixes and Suffixes

Enlist the help of class members in preparing a bulletin board about the use of prefixes and suffixes. Discuss the meaning and use of several common prefixes and suffixes such as pre– (before), anti– (against), mono– (one), bi– (two), dis– (not), re– (again), –ful (full), –fy (to make), –ish (to make an adjective), and –ize (to make a verb). The class should think of three or four words that contain each prefix and suffix, using each one correctly within the context of a sentence. The class may find other prefixes and suffixes and develop their bulletin board utilizing the material just discussed and researched. Colorful yarn, construction paper, and markers are effective, as are descriptive illustrations.

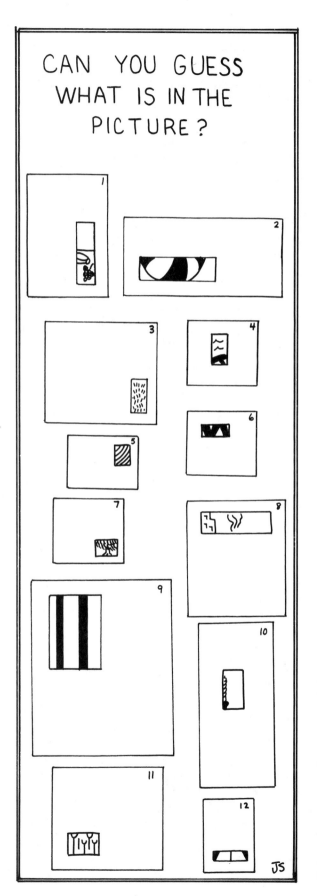

Grades 1–4
Rhyming Answers

Sometimes there are a few minutes of free time at the end of the day. Spend one or two profitable minutes by playing the game "Rhyming Answers." The teacher and the children can write questions on single strips of paper and drop them into a gaily decorated paper bag attached to a bottom corner of a bulletin board. Choose a question from the bag and share it with the class. Call on someone who has thought of a rhyming answer. For example: "Why did it rain so hard today?" "So we couldn't go outside to play"; "Where are you going to put the bat?" "Upon the shelf, on Tommy's hat"; "Where did you find the scissors and glue?" "Under the desk in Sally's shoe."

Grades 2–4
"When I Went Shopping . . ."

To start the game the first child must say, "When I went shopping I bought a (an) *apple*." (The child must choose a word from a category such as food, furniture, books, clothes, toys, household utensils or appliances.) The next person must add a second sentence that describes the object. The third person supplies a sentence that tells how that object will be used. The fourth person must repeat all three sentences. If anyone misses, the next child must be alert and ready to carry on. The ordered sentences may sound something like this: When I went shopping, I bought an apple. It was a red, shiny, juicy one. I'll eat it for lunch.

Grades 3—6
Making Word Associations

Divide the class into three teams. Across the upper part of the chalkboard write the headings *Foreign Language, Science, Art, Social Studies, Music,* and *Mathematics.* On separate slips of paper write words associated with the various fields listed on the chalkboard. Give each class member a word and ask him to write the word under the proper heading. Award two points for each correct response. A list used with sixth graders follows.

masterpiece	quotient	siesta
equation	design	baton
constitution	symphony	Congress
sculpture	minerals	vegetation
bon voyage	numerals	percussion
diplomat	cello	Latin
erosion	etching	suffrage

Grades 3–6
Using Synonym Cards

The teacher or a few students can make up word-meaning games on cards for two children to use. Take the words from vocabulary lists. Arrange each set of four or five words on three-by-five-inch cards cut into strips and keep in small envelopes. Mark the backs of the synonym cards with an identifying symbol such as double lines, stars, circles, etc. Place the words from each envelope across a desk in a single line. One child will try to find the synonym of the first word and place it under the beginning word. (The first word card will have the numeral 1 placed in the upper left-hand corner.) The two synonym cards can be identified correctly by matching the symbols on the card backs. The other child is to keep track of the number of correct responses.

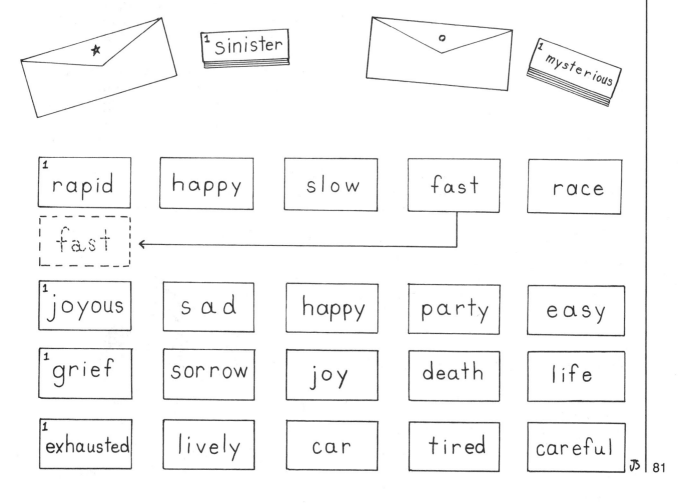

Grades 3–6
Running a Word Relay

On the chalkboard write two columns of ten vocabulary words each, from a recent science or social studies unit. Divide a group of twenty children into two groups. The first person in each group chooses one of the words on the list and, next to it, writes a related word or two. He hurries back to his row, hands the chalk to the next person, and goes to the end of the line. The second person in line walks quickly to the chalkboard, chooses a word on the list and writes a related word next to it, and so on. The action of the game stops when one group finishes. The teacher will decide if each child's related word is correct.

Grades 3–6
Using Word Charades

Divide the class into two teams. From each team member collect a vocabulary word (written on a slip of paper) that could easily be dramatized. Place the words into a team envelope. One child on the team is chosen to pantomime a word taken from the opposite team's envelope. If his team guesses the word within ten seconds, that team is awarded a point. The team that collects the most points wins the game.

Science Vocabulary

kelp – sea plant
hibernation – sleep
terrarium – plants
ptarmigan – Arctic or bird
observe – see
hermit crab – sea animal
tadpoles – frogs
habitat – home
moist – wet
thermometer – temperature

grubs – worms
plankton – algae
mesquite – desert plant
algae – microscopic animals
estivation – resting
aphid – bug
dormancy – inactivity
burrow – hole
vegetarian – eats vegetables
microscope – lens

Grades 4–6
Matching Geographic Names

Record a list of geographic names on heavy oaktag. Use the names of places that the class has already studied. Connect heavy string or yarn to each word in the left-hand column, allowing enough length to reach the correct item to the right. Start the game by dividing the group into two teams. Call someone to the chart to match the first item with the correct answer on the right. A team receives one point for each accurate connection.

It is also possible for only two people to play the game. The first child works the top half of the chart, the second child the bottom half. The teacher checks their responses. A chart developed for a sixth grade follows.

Match the following geographic names:

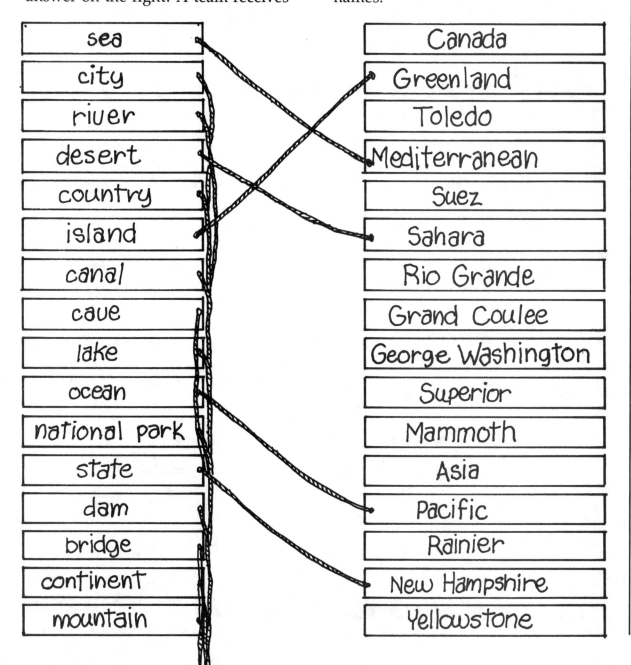

sea	Canada
city	Greenland
river	Toledo
desert	Mediterranean
country	Suez
island	Sahara
canal	Rio Grande
cave	Grand Coulee
lake	George Washington
ocean	Superior
national park	Mammoth
state	Asia
dam	Pacific
bridge	Rainier
continent	New Hampshire
mountain	Yellowstone

Grades 5–6
Suffix-ology

Plan a game with the class using the suffix *–ology*. Explain that *–ology* at the end of a word means *the study of* or *the science of.* Using an experience chart or the chalkboard, write one word at a time and ask the children if they can figure out its meaning. Allow them to use the dictionary if no one knows the meaning. In order to make the game more competitive, divide the class into two groups. Give the group a point if they can answer within a given amount of time. The following words are a few examples of *–ology* words for starting the game:

zoology – animals
bacteriology – bacteria
aerology – air
epidemiology – epidemics
hydrology – water
biology – living things
microbiology – miniature organisms
ecology – organisms and their environment
anthropology – mankind
embryology – embryo and it's development

chronology – time
archaeology – ancient man
graphology – writing
oology – birds' eggs
ecclesiology – church architecture and decoration
geology – earth
entomology – insects

SCORE	
GROUP I	GROUP II
⊩⊩⊩ |||	⊩⊩⊩ ||||

Grades 5–6
Learning Prefixes and Opposites

The whole class or small groups of children can play the following game: The teacher or a specified child says a word containing a prefix, such as the word *disarrange*, and uses it in a sentence. Another child must think of its opposite and use it correctly in a sentence. Other words to use are: dislocate (relocate), undone (done), untie (tie or retie), and unsatisfactory (pleasing or satisfactory).

Grades 1–6
Matching Famous Person with Occupation

Certain children might enjoy creating a matching game, matching the names of famous people and their areas of work. After the children develop their lists, they can mark the names and occupations on strips or cards of oaktag and try to match them correctly. This is a game that can be played at any grade level within any subject area, with modifications in the lists of words. A group of fifth graders might create the following list:

Famous Person	Occupation
Abraham Lincoln	president
Jacques Cousteau	oceanographer
Robert Frost	poet
Albert Einstein	scientist-mathematician
Marco Polo	explorer
Thomas Edison	inventor
Peter Tchaikovsky	composer
Leonard Bernstein	conductor

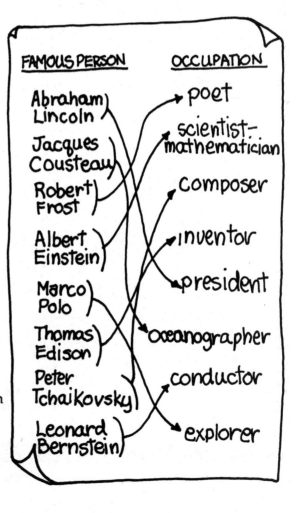

FAMOUS PERSON / OCCUPATION

Abraham Lincoln
Jacques Cousteau
Robert Frost
Albert Einstein
Marco Polo
Thomas Edison
Peter Tchaikovsky
Leonard Bernstein

poet
scientist-mathematician
composer
inventor
president
oceanographer
conductor
explorer

Grade 6
Finding Words Derived
from Famous Names

Before starting the game, place a list of famous names on the chalkboard. Divide the class into two teams and ask them to think of a word originating from each famous name. Award one point for each correct word. The team that collects the most points wins. Examples follow.

Alexander Graham Bell (Bell telephone)

George M. Pullman (pullman or sleeper car on a train)

Ferdinand von Zeppelin (zeppelin or airship)

Louis Pasteur (pasteurization)

Gabriel Fahrenheit (Fahrenheit thermometer)

J. G. Zinn (zinnia flower)

Rudolph Diesel (diesel engine)

Joseph Lister (Listerine antiseptic)

Zebulon Pike (Pike's Peak, Colorado)

J. L. McAdam (macadam road)

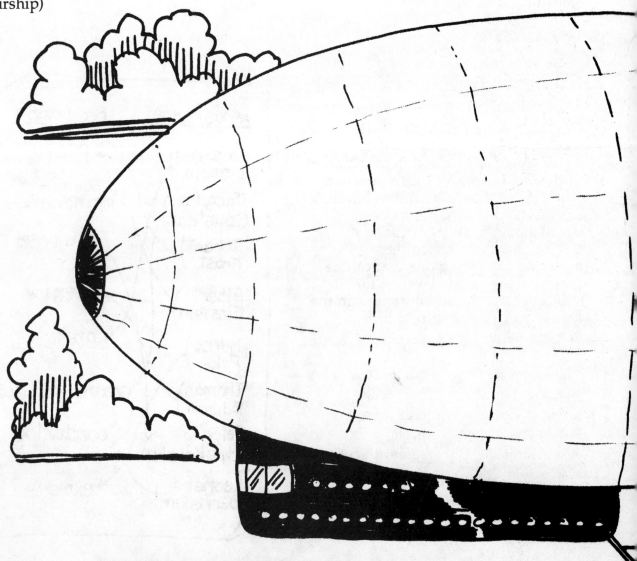

Robert Bunsen (Bunsen burner used in labs)

Jacques Nicot (nicotine)

Anders Celsius (Celsius thermometer)

Samuel F. B. Morse (Morse code used in electric telegraph)

Americus Vespucci (America)

Samuel Colt (Colt revolver)

Louis Braille (Braille printing for the blind)

Hans Geiger (geiger counter)

Isaac Merrit Singer (Singer sewing machine)

Willis H. Carrier (Carrier air conditioning)

Ole Evinrude (Evinrude outboard engine)

O. F. Winchester (Winchester repeating rifle)

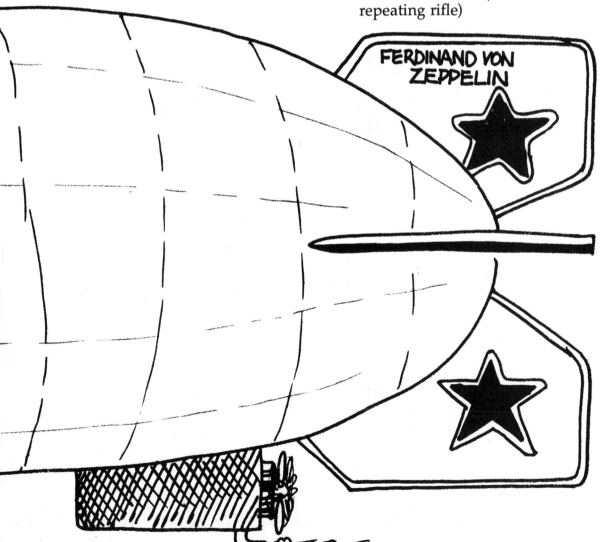

FERDINAND VON ZEPPELIN

CREATIVE WRITING

Grades 3–6
Creating Cartoon Captions

To give children practice in focusing their attention upon a single idea, ask each child in the class to clip three cartoons from newspapers or magazines, cutting off and discarding the captions. After collecting the cartoons in a box, redistribute three cartoons to each person to paste on a piece of construction paper. Each child can create new captions. Collect the cartoons and assemble and fasten the sheets into a booklet for the reading enjoyment of the class.

Grades 3–5
Writing Captions for Cartoons

Encourage the class to collect cartoons for a bulletin board display. After mounting them, ask the children to write captions for any of their choice, then attach these under the proper cartoons. The more appealing cartoons will ultimately have five or six captions attached, while others will have only one.

Grades 4–6
Creating Headlines

Invite the children to bring a newspaper to school and read some of the headlines to the class. Ask the class to write several headlines that might appear in a newspaper twenty-five years from now. Would the headlines concern anyone they know who is their own age?

Grades 3–5
Writing Captions for Animal Pictures

Have the children collect dog and cat pictures or pictures of babies, mount them on colorful construction paper, and create captions for each one. If a bulletin board display of captions is set up outside the classroom, other children in the school would enjoy them as well.

Grades 1–6
Making Alphabet Booklets

Have the children make an alphabet booklet as a class project. Give each student a letter of the alphabet. Ask each child to choose from a special social studies or science unit, one or more words beginning with his letter. The older children can write three or four sentences using each word.

A first grade unit on The Farm might begin with:

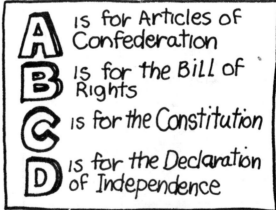

A is for alfalfa
B is for a bushel basket
C is for corn
D is for dairy cattle
E is for eggs

Following is an example of a fifth grade unit on American Independence:

A is for Articles of Confederation
B is for the Bill of Rights
C is for the Constitution
D is for the Declaration of Independence

X and z are usually troublesome. X can be any $x$tra word (any extra word the child wishes to substitute if there are no words beginning with x), and z can be a $z$illion dollar word (any substitute for words beginning with z, preferably unusual or difficult words such as fertilizer or fodder).

Grades 3–6
Writing Picture Titles

To give the class practice in writing short, precise titles for pictures, use the opaque projector to display a wide variety of pictures. As each picture is shown, the children should quickly write a good title for it. Review the pictures again, in order. Take several minutes to discuss each one, and record several of the good titles on the chalkboard for each picture shown. Do not accept generalizations, that is, titles that are not specific.

Grades 3–6
Listing Words for Size

Ask the children to think of words for *big* and *little* to use in writing descriptions.

Big	Little
huge	pint-sized
enormous	tiny
gigantic	minute
lumbering	teensy-weensy
large	child-sized
tall	small
immense	thimble-sized
massive	wee
bulky	puny
mountainous	shrunken
impressive	knee-high
weighty	dwarfish

Grades 1–3
Making a Nonsense-Rhymes Alphabet Book

The children will enjoy making a humorous alphabet book containing two words that rhyme within a single sentence. For example:

The *a*ntelope sat on a cantaloupe.

The *b*at scared the cat.

The *c*at wore a flowery hat.

The *d*og rode a log.

Give each child a letter of the alphabet written on a piece of story paper. Ask each person to write a rhyming sentence about his letter and illustrate it. Collect the papers and make a booklet for the class to enjoy.

Grades 3–6
Creating a Color-words
Ladder

Read a few "color" poems from Mary O'Neill's book *Hailstones and Halibut Bones.* Make a word ladder using color words. Ask, "What is white?" or "What is yellow?" Record the answers in the proper column.

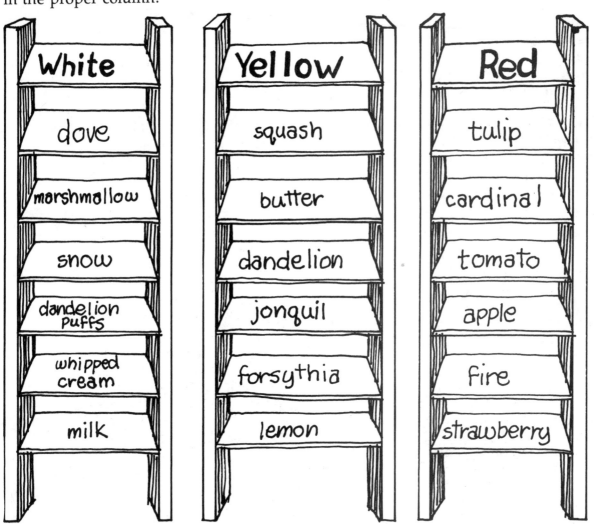

White	Yellow	Red
dove	squash	tulip
marshmallow	butter	cardinal
snow	dandelion	tomato
dandelion puffs	jonquil	apple
whipped cream	forsythia	fire
milk	lemon	strawberry

Hang these word ladders in the classroom for the children to use in their creative writing during the year. For instance, when discussing the use of the simile and the metaphor in writing, a sixth grader might say, "The clouds were as white and fluffy as whipped cream," or, "The clouds, fluffy whipped cream piled high in the sky . . ."

Grades 4–6
Rewriting Ads Using Antonyms

Ask the children to look for interesting ads in magazines or newspapers that contain many descriptive words. Each child should either think of antonyms for these words or find the antonyms in a dictionary or a thesaurus. Rewrite the ads using the antonyms. When they have finished, students can share the hilarious results with their classmates by making posters with the cut-out objects and new words.

Grades 4–6
Listing Action Words
in Hobbies

Ask each child to choose a hobby or special interest he enjoys, then list all the action words that he uses in his hobby. Using sewing as an example, the following words apply:

Sewing

cut (the material)	clip (the collar)
stitch (the seams)	hem (the skirt)
fit (the bodice)	thread (the needle)
match (the tabs)	operate (the sewing machine)

Illustrated words will make a more interesting, attractive page. Using the action words on each person's list, write a description of that hobby. Collect the pages and arrange into a class booklet, or display the pages on a bulletin board.

Grades 2–5
Using Action Words
in Place of *Go*

Encourage the class to think of alternate ways to express action words such as *go*. First, make a list on the chalkboard of as many things as the children can remember that *go*. The list might include the nouns *planes, horses, cars,* and *insects*. Take a word from the list such as *plane* and write applicable verbs in place of *go*. For example:

Planes	Horses	Cars	Insects
land	tramp	function	crawl
bank	trot	race	slither
fly	gallop	zoom	fly
glide	step	speed	swim
soar	buck	pass	invade
turn	lope	careen	hop

Grades 1–3
Having a Sale of Words

Read "Longbeard the Wizard" by Sid Fleischman to the class, then have your own sale of words, using color words, how-to words, and others. Collect them in shoeboxes, envelopes, or empty juice cans decorated with wallpaper. Use these words in writing descriptive sentences together.

Grades 3–6
Making Action–word Ladders

Using shelfpaper, make long ladders of action words. Hang paper from the ceiling to the floor. Children can easily add to these ladders by writing on the shelfpaper. Have them write ladder lists of words for *blow, fall,* and *see*. As the class works on each list, ask, "What can blow?" "The wind." "How does the wind blow?" "It whistles." "It shrieks." Record the words *whistle* and *shriek* in the *Blow* column. Continue this line of questioning for each column. The children will use these lists in their creative writing. A possible list follows.

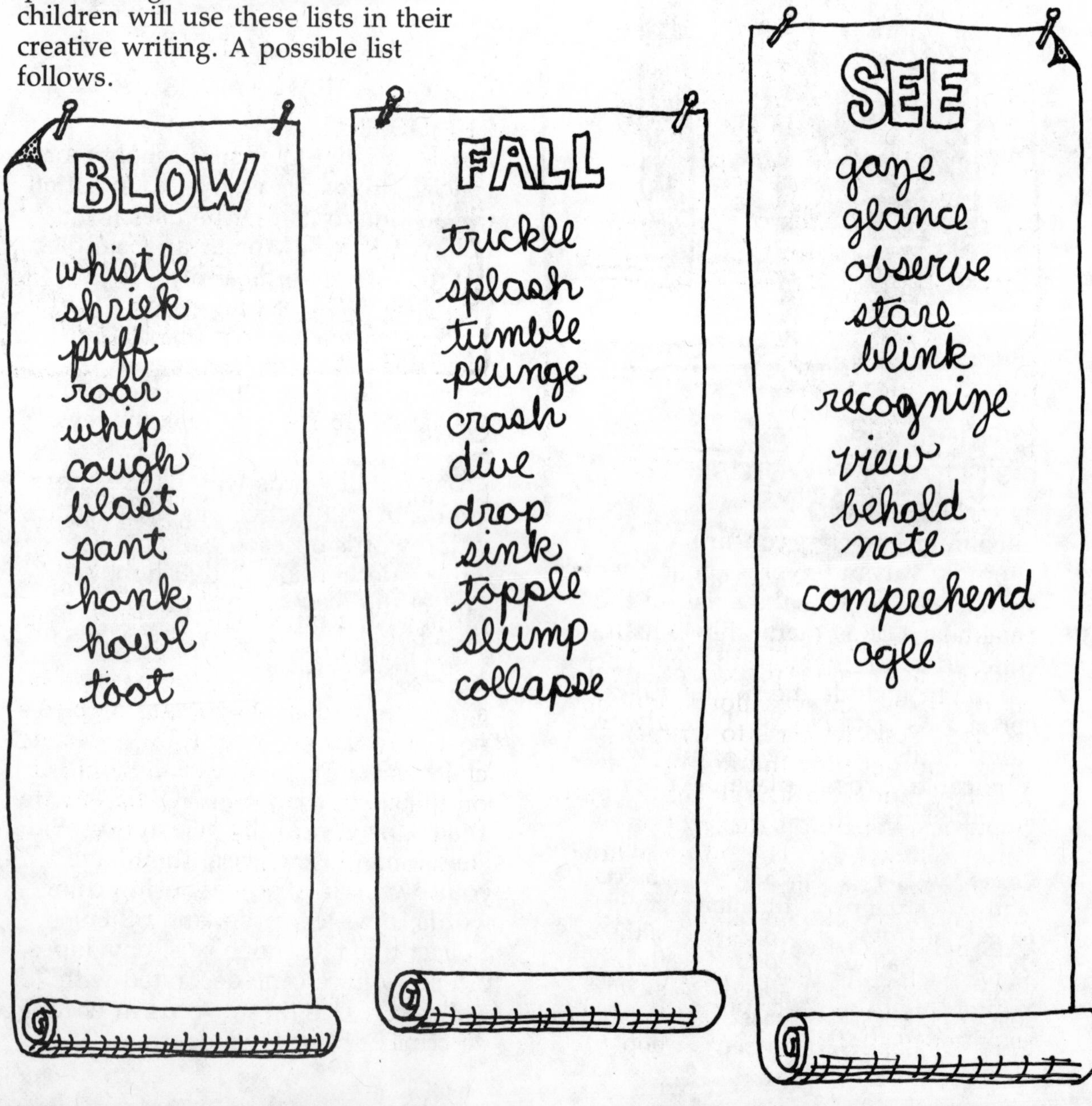

BLOW

whistle
shriek
puff
roar
whip
cough
blast
pant
honk
howl
toot

FALL

trickle
splash
tumble
plunge
crash
dive
drop
sink
topple
slump
collapse

SEE

gaze
glance
observe
stare
blink
recognize
view
behold
note
comprehend
ogle

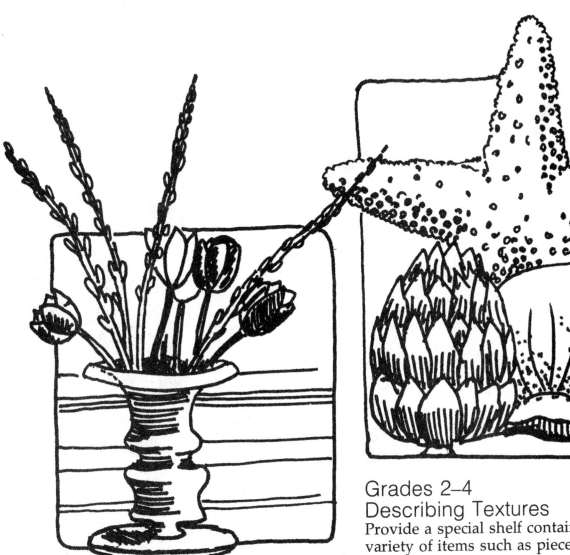

Grades 1–6
Writing Flower Descriptions

On a desk or table, place a bouquet of tulips, roses, pussy willows, jonquils, or lilacs. Ask the class to write a description of how the flowers look and feel, and what the flowers remind them of. One child's description of pussy willows is: "The pussy willows are as gray as a rainy sky, and feel soft and furry like my kitten." Use an experience chart with grades 1 and 2. Have each child draw a picture and copy one of the descriptions from the experience chart.

Grades 2–4
Describing Textures

Provide a special shelf containing a variety of items such as pieces of cloth of various textures, a sponge, a rubber eraser, a chamois, a piece of cardboard, a pine cone, a spruce twig, a seashell, a piece of coral, a vegetable brush, a vegetable (such as a piece of lettuce or a potato), a bird's nest, a rose, and other things. Let the children touch the objects assembled on the shelf, then prepare charts with the children's simple descriptive phrases and drawings. Some examples of children's phrases are:

a velvety flower petal

a ridged, honeycombed piece of coral

slippery, smooth satin

sharp, pointed bristles

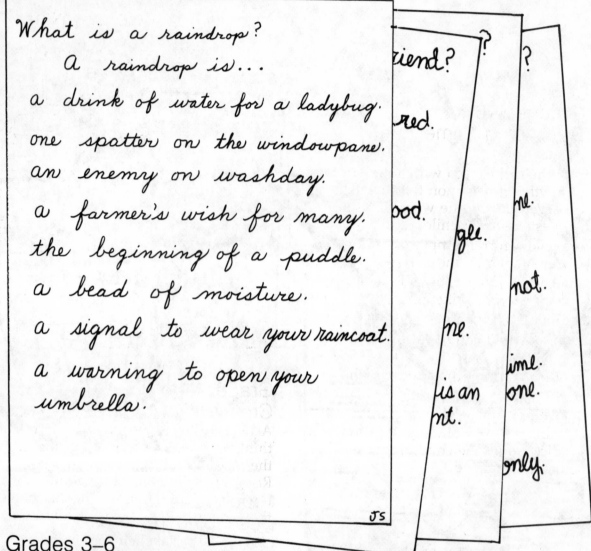

What is a raindrop?
   A raindrop is...
a drink of water for a ladybug.
one spatter on the windowpane.
an enemy on washday.
a farmer's wish for many.
the beginning of a puddle.
a bead of moisture.
a signal to wear your raincoat.
a warning to open your umbrella.

Grades 3–6
Making Posters
of Descriptive Phrases

Divide the class into groups of three or four. Have each group develop a poster by using words, phrases, or sentences to answer a question written on the poster. One group might work on the question: What is summer?

hot, scorching days
running over hot sandy beaches
no school
fun
trips
sleeping late

Other questions for a group to answer on a poster are
What is a raindrop?
What is a friend?
What is a report card?
What is a cloud?
What is a mother?
What is a dog?

Grades 3–6
Describing Something in Motion

Ask the children to write a description of anything in motion that they observed during the week. Possible suggestions from children include:

an agile squirrel jumping from one tree branch to another

the cheerful paperboy delivering papers on his bike

a robin building a nest

a six-year-old child learning to ride a bike

mother washing the supper dishes

an icy snowball whizzing through the air

Variation: Write the description as a riddle and let the children guess what is being described.

Grades 4–6
Creating Descriptive Phrases

As a class project, ask the children to think of different ways of looking at the moon (or at faces, snowflakes). Record the different descriptions under each title. Display the charts on the wall or bulletin board. Children create such examples as

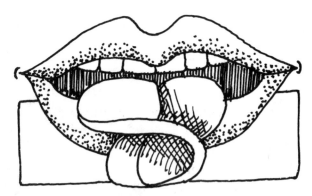

Grades 3–6
Tongue Twisters

Use a child's name such as Tim. Then think of a word to describe Tim, starting with a *t* (Tiny Tim). Ask what Tim can do, using *t* words (Tiny Tim twists his tongue ten times). Children enjoy this activity. Allow them to listen to each other's creations.

((MOON))

• a pearl on black velvet

• a king of all the nighttime heavenly bodies

• man's steppingstone into space

• a bright shining beacon

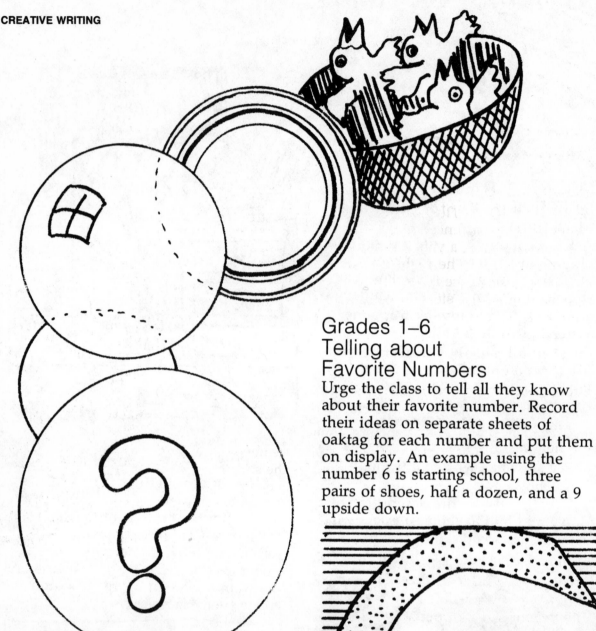

Grades 1–6
Telling about
Favorite Numbers

Urge the class to tell all they know about their favorite number. Record their ideas on separate sheets of oaktag for each number and put them on display. An example using the number 6 is starting school, three pairs of shoes, half a dozen, and a 9 upside down.

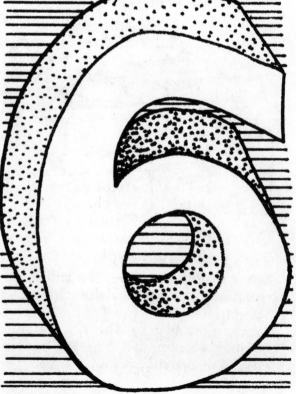

Grades 1–6
Circle Images

Draw a circle on the board, then ask the class to imagine what they see in the circle, for example, an icy, wet, white snowball; a nest of baby birds with beaks wide open; nickels, dimes, and quarters; an owl's eye; or my mother's shimmering china plates.

Ask the children to list as many images as they can imagine, then collect the lists. Invite a group of children to construct a bulletin board with accompanying drawings, using any ideas on the lists.

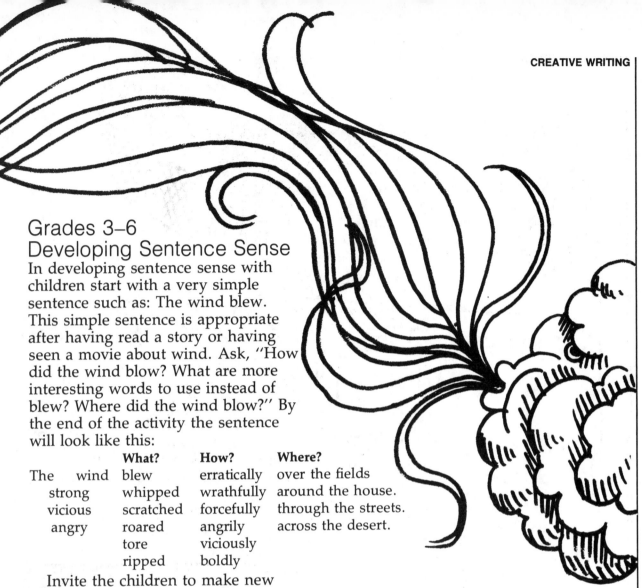

Grades 3–6
Developing Sentence Sense

In developing sentence sense with children start with a very simple sentence such as: The wind blew. This simple sentence is appropriate after having read a story or having seen a movie about wind. Ask, "How did the wind blow? What are more interesting words to use instead of blew? Where did the wind blow?" By the end of the activity the sentence will look like this:

	What?	**How?**	**Where?**
The wind	blew	erratically	over the fields
strong	whipped	wrathfully	around the house.
vicious	scratched	forcefully	through the streets.
angry	roared	angrily	across the desert.
	tore	viciously	
	ripped	boldly	

Invite the children to make new sentences using the lists of words:

The strong wind tore forcefully around the house.

The vicious wind ripped angrily over the fields.

The angry wind roared erratically through the streets.

Next, ask the children if the sentences could be changed so that the word "the" does not appear at the beginning. Let the children experiment orally. Record anything that makes sense or sounds good. Some children's examples are:

Scratching and roaring, the angry wind whipped erratically through the streets.

Boldly the strong wind tore around the house.

Over the fields ripped the angry wind.

Grades 1–6
Writing Sentences:
Field Trip Experiences

Take pictures of the children during field trips. Also allow the children to take pictures with the class camera provided by the teacher. Have the children write a sentence or two describing what is happening in the picture. A small group of interested children can place the pictures and written descriptions, in sequence, in a booklet. The finished product will be a story of their field trip.

Grades 3–6
Developing Sentences
from Categories

Use a long sheet of shelfpaper and
divide it into categories. Have the
children think of words under each
category. When finished have fun
putting words from each category into
a sentence.

DETERMINERS	COLOR WORDS	SIZE WORDS	WHAT MOOD	THINGS AND PEOPLE
the	silvery	gigantic	grouchy	fish
many	glowing	enormous	happy	bride
a	puckery	tiny	frustrated	lemon
an	beautiful	large	delighted	car
hundreds	shiny	huge	active	seamstress
numerous	pretty	micro-scopic	puzzled	panda
			pensive	basket
			angry	needle

The sentences can make sense as well as being nonsensical when the chart is completed.

1. Numerous silvery, tiny, active fish swam swiftly yesterday.
2. Hundreds of puckery, enormous, grouchy lemons fell softly in church last week.
3. Many shiny, large, puzzled cars crashed loudly on the road on Sunday.
4. A puckery, gigantic, grouchy bride cried belligerently in the air years ago.

ACTION WORDS	HOW WORDS	WHERE WORDS	WHEN WORDS
fell	swiftly	on the road	yesterday
smiled	Loudly	in church	on Sunday
cried	softly	at the store	tomorrow
swam	abruptly	at the beach	years ago
tiptoed	belligerently	in the air	some day
crashed	carefully	overhead	last week

Grades 2–5
Writing a Sentence

Ask the class to take turns going to the window. After the children have worked with sentences, have them make up a sentence about what they saw as they looked out the window, but tell them they should not begin the sentence with "I see" or "I saw." Examples:

A bright red cardinal flew past the window.

Leaves are falling.

A puddle of water is sitting in the middle of the sidewalk.

A jet trail streaks the sky.

Shadows spread across the playground.

Grades 3–6
Rearranging Words and Phrases

Have the class arrange words and phrases, placed on cards, into meaningful sentences. Ask the children to rearrange them several different ways.

| The brown leaves | fell | to the ground |

| because it was windy | yesterday |

Because it was windy, the brown leaves fell to the ground yesterday.
Yesterday the brown leaves fell to the ground, because it was windy.
Yesterday, because it was windy, the brown leaves fell to the ground.

| Mother took us | to the park | last Sunday |

| because it was a warm, sunny day. |

Because it was a warm, sunny day last Sunday, Mother took us to the park.
Last Sunday Mother took us to the park, because it was a warm, sunny day.

Other sentences to rearrange:

| I rode my bike | to school | today | so I wouldn't be late |

| Tom broke his leg | while skiing | in Vermont | last week. |

| He swam | across the pool | in thirty seconds |

| while competing in a race. |

Grades 3–5
Developing a Sentence
for a Picture Post Card

Give each child or each small group a colorful or interesting picture post card. Have them write a descriptive sentence of the scene. As a variation, ask the children to bring pictures showing something happening, then ask them to write a sentence describing the action on a three-by-five-inch card. A couple of children could attach the cards in the central area of a bulletin board, arranging the pictures in a square or circle around the descriptions. Attach yarn to each card. Later, as a small group activity, ask a child to read a description card and attach the yarn to the proper picture.

Grades 3–4
Creating Sentences
for Pictures

Ask individual children to cut pictures from newspapers and magazines, then write a descriptive sentence for each picture. Explain that the sentence must accurately describe the principal concept or idea of the picture. A booklet can be prepared to display individual work.

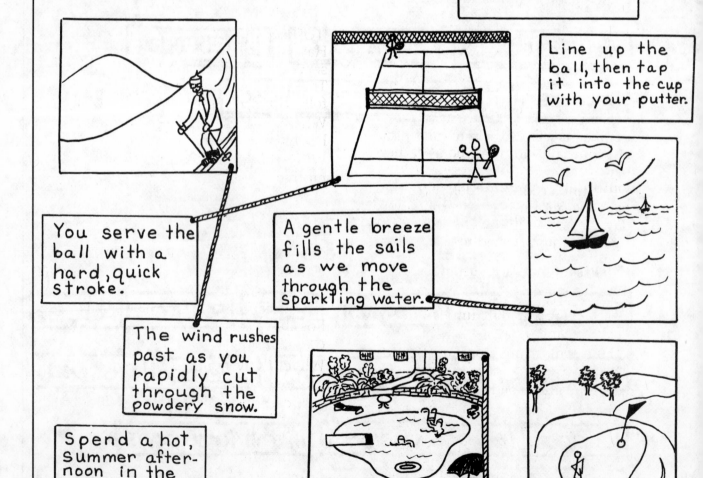

Match the description card with the correct picture.

Line up the ball, then tap it into the cup with your putter.

You serve the ball with a hard, quick stroke.

A gentle breeze fills the sails as we move through the sparkling water.

The wind rushes past as you rapidly cut through the powdery snow.

Spend a hot, summer afternoon in the pool.

Grades 3–6
Creating Colorful, Descriptive Sentences

After the children have had practice in writing descriptive words for nouns, let them write colorful, descriptive sentences by completing two or three of the following phrases:

1. He had just started to doze when suddenly . . .

2. Angrily he slammed down the phone when . . .

3. The huge boulder rumbled nearer and nearer as . . .

4. He wrinkled his nose in distaste as . . .

5. As the snake slithered closer . . .

Some children may want to develop several descriptive sentences from one idea. Introduce the preceding activity by having each child open a library book, find a very descriptive sentence, and share it with the rest of the class.

Grades 3–6
Developing Sentences from a Simple Sentence

Have the children give you a basic sentence such as: Clouds drift. Then ask them to answer the following questions:

Where do the clouds drift? (in the heavens)

When do the clouds drift? (from morning to dusk)

How do they drift? (lazily)

Why do they drift? (to blot out the sun)

Give some color words to describe the clouds. (white, fluffy)

Ask the class to develop a variety of sentences from the basic sentence. Possible examples are:

Clouds drift.

White, fluffy clouds drift lazily from morning to dusk.

Clouds drift in the heavens to blot out the sun.

Lazily white, fluffy clouds drift to blot out the sun.

From morning to dusk clouds drift lazily.

Grades 3–6
Creating a Catchy Sentence

After reading a story to the class, such as "Little Princess Goodnight" by Bill Martin, make up a catchy sentence. Record the sentence on the chalkboard or use shelfpaper for a more permanent record. An example of such a sentence is:

The	peacock	crept	out	from under	the chair
	fox	yelled	under		the step
	clown	slipped	into		the hole
	father	escaped	over		the fence

and	pinched	the	dragon	under the bed.
	tickled		policeman	on the nose.
	squeezed		gumdrop	among the weeds.
	juggled		magician	over his head.

As the class thinks of something else to name in place of the peacock, ask them to list at least half a dozen names. Continue to substitute words for nouns, verbs, prepositions, etc. Read the new sentences the class develops from the substitutions and have a good laugh. Children also love doing this activity by themselves or in small groups. Some substitute sentences in the style of the preceding example are

The fox yelled under the step and tickled the policeman on the nose.

The clown slipped into the hole and squeezed the gumdrop among the weeds.

Father escaped over the fence and juggled the magician over his head.

After enjoying the fanciful sentences created, try organizing a sensible one following the same example.

The next day, as a follow-up activity, read to the class a short ghost story, such as "What's a Ghost Going to Do?" by Jane Thayer. Have the children get into groups of four or five and use the following sentence: The ghost floated through the deserted house and rattled some chains in the attic. Choose a responsible person in each group to record the substitutions the children create. When each group has concluded the activity, have them move into a large group again and share the sentences each group has created.

Grades 3–6
Developing a Sentence
Using Action Words

Place the headings *Who, Action Words, How, Where,* and *When* on the chalkboard. Make a list of action words used in car racing or other activities. After the list has been written on the chalkboard under the *Action Words* column, ask the following questions:

1. *Who* might do these activities?
2. *How* might he do it?
3. *Where* did he do it?
4. *When* did it happen?

Record a variety of answers under the appropriate column. The list developed may look something like this:

Ask each child to choose a word or phrase from each column, developing a sentence of his own, then read it to the class. Sentence possibilities are:

Bobby Allison's car skidded dangerously across the track during the race.

The driver threw the clutch quickly into second gear when the race started.

My brother bounced his car crazily against the wall during the second lap.

Al Unser cleverly squeezed past a car on the straightaway near the end of the race.

WHO	ACTION WORDS	HOW	WHERE	WHEN
driver	skidded	crazily	across the track	during the race
brother	threw the clutch	quickly	into second gear	at the end of the race
Bobby Allison	bounced his car	cleverly	on the straightaway	when the race started
Al Unser	squeezed past a car	dangerously	against the wall	during the second lap

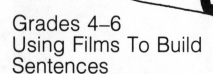

Grades 4–6
Using Films To Build Sentences

Films motivate a class to develop good descriptive sentences. The film "Waterfalls" contains ample material for development. After viewing the film, the children can (1) make a list of action words describing the waterfall (plunging, striking, swelling, showering, pouring, roaring, foaming, thundering, descending). It is more interesting to do this orally with the class, recording their ideas on the chalkboard or on shelfpaper; (2) make comparisons of various aspects of the waterfall: as wide as . . ., as foamy as . . ., as loud as . . ., like a roaring lion, like a thundering herd of wild buffalo; (3) record any descriptive phrases the children create: explosions of mist and vapor, veils of mist, roared rapidly over a slippery jumble of cascading rocks; and (4) write some descriptive sentences about the waterfall. The children can use any of the preceding words or phrases in the sentence, adding any ideas of their own. Expect some good sentences.

Like a thundering herd of wild buffalo, the water pounded the smooth rocks below.

The water below the showering falls looked as foamy as soapsuds.

Swifty the water cascaded from the edge of the brown, slippery rocks.

The waterfall, roaring and pouring over the edge into space, plunged headlong into the pool below.

Use the preceding sentences as models if the children have any trouble getting started with their own ideas.

Grades 4–6
Writing Conversations

Magazines abound in pictures showing two or more people talking in a lively manner. Direct each child to attach a magazine picture to a piece of notebook paper, choose a partner, then work with him to write conversations for both their pictures. To set the proper mood, let the class role-play their pictures before actually writing their conversations.

Grades 4–6
Varying Structure of Conversation

Discuss the use of variation in writing conversations. Examples of inverted order and sentence division are:

"We must hurry, or we'll miss the bus," she explained.

She explained, "We must hurry, or we'll miss the bus."

"We must hurry," she explained, "or we'll miss the bus."

Grades 4–6
Finding Interesting
First Sentences

Ask the class to find interesting first sentences from a variety of materials such as newspaper accounts or stories found in library books, paperbacks, magazines, and pamphlets. After these lists of sentences and phrases have been recorded on a chart, suggest that the class write paragraphs or very short stories, utilizing some favorite passage on the chart. Possibilities for first sentences or beginning phrases follow.

By a fateful coincidence . . .

At four o'clock in the afternoon on December 2, 1863, Susan boldly . . .

Softly the rain fell.

They had been in the cave two weeks when . . .

It was a sticky, hot summer day in 1917 . . .

In the ordinary course of things, Abraham Tidwell was not a friend of mine.

"Are you awake?" Andy anxiously asked his father.

There was still an hour of daylight left when . . .

Years ago, when the seventeen-year locusts . . .

Just above the crest of the hill I saw . . .

About twenty miles to the north of the accident site . . .

Grades 4–6
Substituting Phrases
in Written Conversation

Have the class think of a variety of phrases to use instead of the common "she said" and "he said" frequently employed in written conversations. Record their responses on an experience chart, to be used in their creative writing. Give the children a few examples such as:

he sighed	she yawned
she repeated	she nodded
argued Steve	he shouted
Dave remembered	she cried angrily

As the children find new ones during their reading, add them to the chart.

The class can then find other words for "he asked" and "she asked" when used in conversations asking questions. The following substitutes lend variety to questions:

she requested	pleaded the witness
probed the judge	he explored
questioned Sam	she pursued

Encourage boys and girls to use these new phrases in their creative writing.

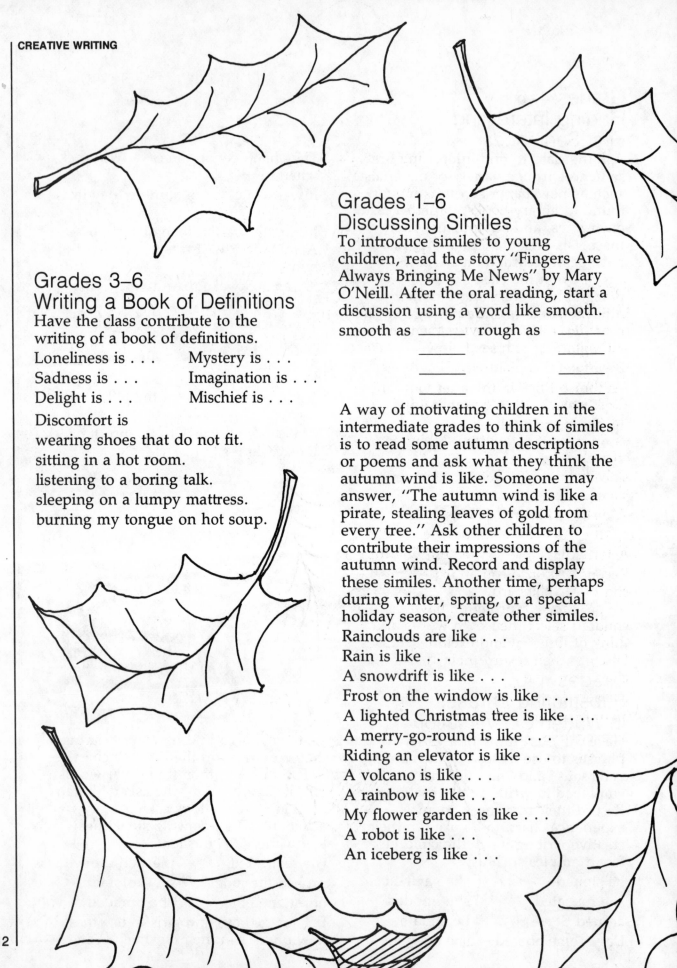

Grades 3–6
Writing a Book of Definitions

Have the class contribute to the writing of a book of definitions.

Loneliness is . . .   Mystery is . . .

Sadness is . . .   Imagination is . . .

Delight is . . .   Mischief is . . .

Discomfort is

wearing shoes that do not fit.

sitting in a hot room.

listening to a boring talk.

sleeping on a lumpy mattress.

burning my tongue on hot soup.

Grades 1–6
Discussing Similes

To introduce similes to young children, read the story "Fingers Are Always Bringing Me News" by Mary O'Neill. After the oral reading, start a discussion using a word like smooth.

smooth as _____   rough as _____

_____   _____

_____   _____

_____   _____

A way of motivating children in the intermediate grades to think of similes is to read some autumn descriptions or poems and ask what they think the autumn wind is like. Someone may answer, "The autumn wind is like a pirate, stealing leaves of gold from every tree." Ask other children to contribute their impressions of the autumn wind. Record and display these similes. Another time, perhaps during winter, spring, or a special holiday season, create other similes.

Rainclouds are like . . .

Rain is like . . .

A snowdrift is like . . .

Frost on the window is like . . .

A lighted Christmas tree is like . . .

A merry-go-round is like . . .

Riding an elevator is like . . .

A volcano is like . . .

A rainbow is like . . .

My flower garden is like . . .

A robot is like . . .

An iceberg is like . . .

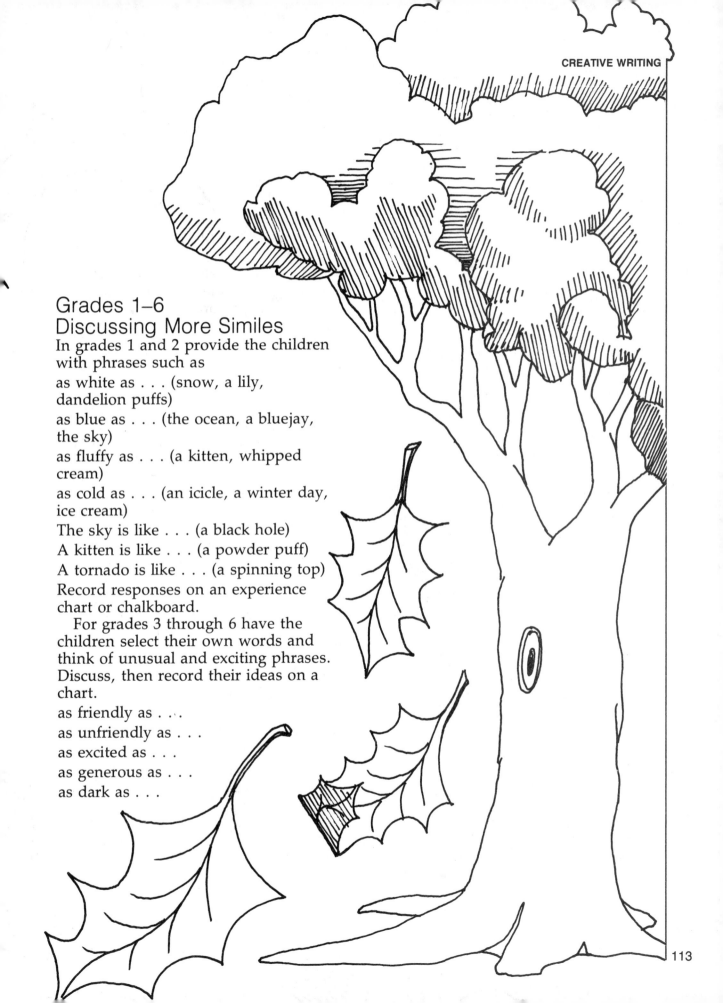

Grades 1–6
Discussing More Similes

In grades 1 and 2 provide the children with phrases such as

as white as . . . (snow, a lily, dandelion puffs)

as blue as . . . (the ocean, a bluejay, the sky)

as fluffy as . . . (a kitten, whipped cream)

as cold as . . . (an icicle, a winter day, ice cream)

The sky is like . . . (a black hole)

A kitten is like . . . (a powder puff)

A tornado is like . . . (a spinning top)

Record responses on an experience chart or chalkboard.

For grades 3 through 6 have the children select their own words and think of unusual and exciting phrases. Discuss, then record their ideas on a chart.

as friendly as . . .

as unfriendly as . . .

as excited as . . .

as generous as . . .

as dark as . . .

Grades 4–6
Creating Sentences
with Similes
With the help of the class, make a list of things that can be seen, and describe each thing imaginatively.

We see	We imagine
clouds	powder puffs
snowdrift	mountain
trail of ants	soldiers marching in line
fire	hungry tongues lapping the air

After giving them an example or two, ask the children to try using the words in sentences.

1. The clouds, like fluffy powder puffs, drifted slowly across the sky.
2. The enormous snowdrift, like a mountain, curved gently across the yard.
3. Like soldiers marching in line, the trail of ants moved across my kitchen floor.
4. The fire, like hungry tongues lapping the air, ate everything in its path.

Grades 2–3
"I Would Like to Be . . ."
Read to the children "Why Can't I Be William?" by Ellen Conford. Ask the class, "Did any of you ever wish to be like someone else you know?" Allow time for discussion. Invite them to write a few lines beginning "I would like to be . . .," giving reasons for their choice.

Grades 4–6
Discussing "Casey at the Bat"
During the World Series play-offs, the class will enjoy hearing the poem "Casey at the Bat" by Ernest Thayer. After the reading, ask the following questions:

What does the bat do? (whizzes, zooms, flies, catapults, lobs, slams, slaps, smashes)

Where does the ball go? (over the fence, into the stands, into a mitt, out of the ball park, out to left field)

Ask other questions about the people in the stands, the ball park, or any other associated ideas. Write descriptive words and phrases on the chalkboard. After the discussion, ask the interested children to write about the bat, the ball, the stands, or the people, using some of the words and phrases listed on the chalkboard.

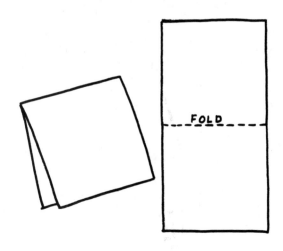

Grades 1–6
Creating Get-well Cards
When a child has been absent from school for several days, provide a variety of art materials for the children to create get-well cards for the sick classmate. Teach the children a variety of ways to fold the paper.

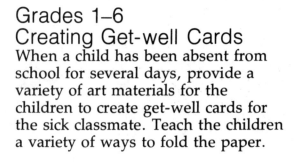

JS

Grades 1–2
Developing Sentences through Letter Writing

Encourage the class to write a class letter to a sick child. Use an experience chart with first- or second-grade children. Calling for ideas from the children, record the activities that have occurred during the week. When the letter is completed, the class members can sign their names to it. Fold the letter, put it into a large manila envelope, and send the letter with a child who lives near the absentee.

Grades 2–5
Developing Sentences from a Picture

Have the class cut pictures from magazines of people with various expressions and write a sentence or two about each one, telling how each person feels or what he is thinking.

Grades 3–5
Developing a Paragraph about Fall

Read some fall poems, then ask each child to think of a sentence about fall. Choose five children to go to the front of the class and recite their sentences, one after another. Listen to how they sound. Ask the class to help rearrange the five children so that the sentences form a coherent paragraph. Listen to them recite their sentences again. Repeat this procedure with five new children.

Grades 3–6
Developing a Paragraph about a Special Topic

Suggest that the children write a paragraph about one of the following:
If I were a teacher . . .

> the president . . .
> a king . . .
> a giraffe . . .
> a cat . . .
> a pencil . . .

Grades 1–5
Describing Yards

Read "Joseph's Yard" by Charles Keeping to the class, then ask them to describe what is in their yards. After the discussion, ask the children to write a descriptive sentence, paragraph, or story about their yards. Those who are interested could use cameras, take pictures of their yards, then develop descriptive stories around their pictures. Another topic for a follow-up activity is "What I See from My Window" or "What I See from a Train Window."

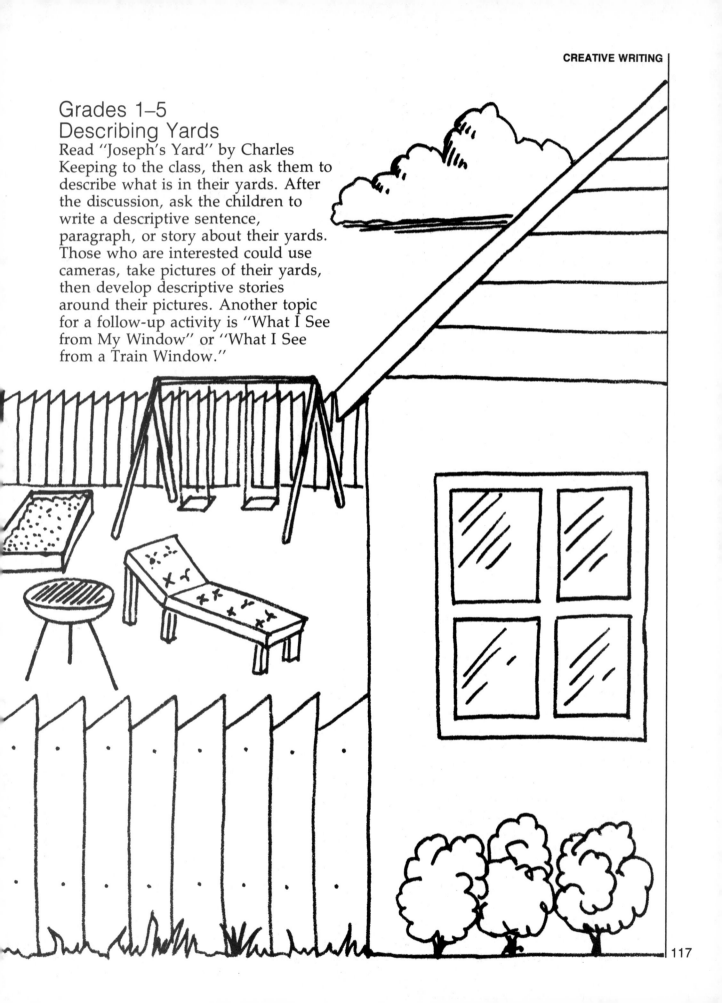

117

Grades 1–3
Creating Silly Pictures and Stories

Invite the children to create silly pictures and make up silly stories to go with their pictures. First graders can dictate their stories to the teacher or an aide, then share them with the class.

Grades 3–6
Creating a Title and Topic Sentence

Ask the children to bring a magazine, library book, or newspaper to class the next day. Have them write the title and first sentence of an interesting story. Record five or six of the most intriguing topics on the chalkboard. The class can then choose one of these to finish as a paragraph.

Grades 3–6
Developing a Paragraph from a Picture

Suggest that the children bring in several interesting pictures cut from magazines or newspapers. Mount them on colorful construction paper in class. Allow each child to choose a picture and write a paragraph describing what is happening in the picture. Build a bulletin board using each picture and paragraph.

Another activity using the same pictures is to have the class write newspaper headlines or captions to accompany each picture and arrange them on the bulletin board.

Grades 1–6
Writing a Paragraph of Favorite Sounds

After reading from Mary O'Neill's book *What Is That Sound!* talk about sounds the children heard in the poems. Using favorite sounds as the main idea of discussion, have the children think about *their* favorite sounds. Make a list of them on the chalkboard. A sample list follows.

sounds of morning—birds chirping, radio blaring, alarm clock buzzing, kids yelling

sounds of downtown—cars honking, feet shuffling, brakes screeching, bus engines roaring

sounds of the beach—waves lapping, seagulls calling

sounds in the kitchen—toaster popping, bacon sizzling

night sounds—owl hooting, crickets chirping, frogs croaking

construction sounds—hammers pounding, machines sputtering

The children can write their own paragraphs about the topic "My Favorite Sounds" using some of the *sound* words. First or second graders could pick a *sounds* topic and create a paragraph on the experience chart, the teacher recording their sentences. Fifth and sixth graders would enjoy tape-recording sounds to use as a background to the reading of their paragraphs.

Grades 1–3
Writing Funny Stories Using Pairs of Rhyming Words

Collect pairs of rhyming words from the children and record them on the chalkboard. Examples: rock-dock, lucky-ducky, silly-Billy, bad-lad, queer-deer, quick-stick. Ask what might happen to a quick-stick, or a bad-lad, and so on. Have the children utilize several of the funny words when writing their stories. In the case of first graders, write a class story together on an experience chart.

Grades 3–4
Making Up Spider Stories

Instruct the class: Imagine that you are spiders on the way to the moon in a rocket ship. Are you able to spin a web? How do you feel? What do you see? Write a story about your adventure.

Grades 1–4
Reporting Unusual Happenings

During the week, curious, funny, or unusual things happen in the room or on the playground. If a dog runs off with a sweater on the playground, write about it. If a butterfly emerges from its cocoon and rests on a child's desk, write about it. For first or second graders, these experiences are best written on chart paper as a class story. Third and fourth graders may enjoy writing their own versions of the incident.

Grades 3–6
Writing a Funny Mystery

The class can write a funny story about something mysterious or out of the ordinary happening at home or at school. For idea starters, ask such questions as: What happened to the front tire of your bike? What became of your right-hand glove? Where did that puddle of water in the middle of the kitchen floor come from? Who put the baseball cap in the refrigerator? How did baby brother's shoe get in Mother's large pan?

Grades 3–6
Being Aware on
the Way to School

"Describe something you saw on your way to school today." This is an open assignment for anytime during the year when some special scene or happening inspires a child. Encourage the children to take a picture with a camera, then write their paragraphs or stories.

Grades 5–6
Introducing Bicentennial Treasures

Make a list of the nation's bicentennial treasures. Add other valued possessions to the list.

Declaration of Independence	Liberty Bell
U.S. Constitution	Statue of Liberty
Bill of Rights	First Flag

Ask the children to create one of these cherished possessions in one of the following ways.

poster: felt marker, tempera, crayon

picture: watercolor, crayon, tempera, pastels

sculpture: clay, play dough*

diarama

Attach a five- by-eight-inch card on which is written a descriptive paragraph of the object

*Play Dough Recipe:

Mix together 3 cups flour and ¾ cup salt

Add water (as needed to moisten)

Add food coloring, 5 to 10 drops or dry tempera, 1 to 3 teaspoons

Knead, add a little flour if too sticky, and place in a plastic bag or covered jar. Will keep in a cool place for several weeks.

Grades 4–6
Analyzing Character Traits

There are many stories for teachers to select that contain characters endowed with definite traits. After reading such a story to the children, discuss the traits of two of the central characters. If you read "From the Mixed-up Files of Mrs. Basil E. Frankweiler" by E. Konigsburg, analyze the characteristics of Claudia and Jamie. Follow up with a creative writing activity: "Why I Would Like Claudia (or Jamie) As a Friend." Perhaps a child would prefer writing "Why I Wouldn't Like Claudia (or Jamie) as a Friend."

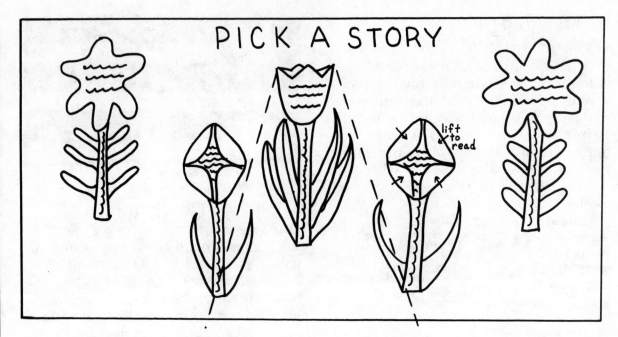

PICK A STORY

lift
to
read

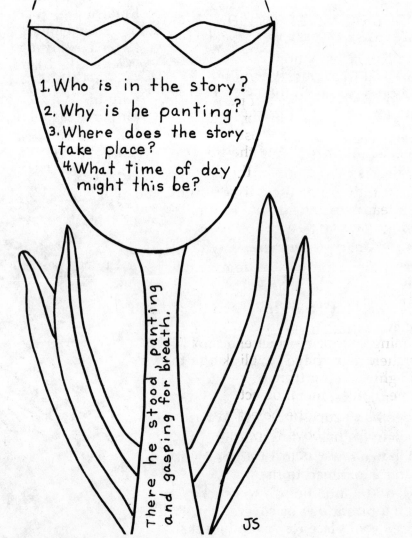

1. Who is in the story?
2. Why is he panting?
3. Where does the story take place?
4. What time of day might this be?

There he stood panting and gasping for breath.

JS

Grades 5–6
Picking a Story

Teachers can prepare a garden of story ideas on a large bulletin board. Using a variety of flowers and plants made from colored construction paper, attach a topic sentence to the stem. Questions concerning the story can be attached to several flowers. Invite the class to pick a story topic from the garden. To help you start planting story ideas for your bulletin board, pick a few from the following examples:

Jeff was swimming for the diving raft when he heard a call for help.
1. Who was calling for help?
2. Did he reach the person in time to save him?
3. What other people were involved in the rescue?
4. What finally happened?

As Sue reached for the old pewter teapot she had found in her grandmother's attic, she lost her balance and knocked it to the floor.
1. What was she doing in the attic?
2. What treasure did she discover in the teapot?
3. What did she do with it?
4. Did Sue tell anyone about her discovery?

Paul and his friend Bob were camping in the backyard one night when they were awakened by an intense humming sound. As they emerged from their tent, they saw blinking blue lights coming from a strange-looking metal object.
1. How large was the object?
2. What did the boys discover?
3. Where did the object come from?
4. What happened to the boys?

There he stood, panting and gasping for breath.
1. Who is in the story?
2. Why is he panting?
3. Where does the story take place?
4. What time of day might this be?

Steve awakened suddenly from a deep sleep. He heard a thunderous crash, and saw zigzags of lightning cut the sky.
1. Where is Steve?
2. Who else might be in this story?
3. When might this have happened?
4. Did the lightning strike anything nearby?

Take a few minutes for discussion before the class starts writing about a chosen topic. Explain that the topic sentences they picked are to be used at the beginning of their stories or utilized within the context of their stories. The questions attached to the leaves are guides to help them develop ideas for the story line. The children will add their own creative details to complete the story.

Grades 3–4
Writing about Foreign Lands

Read about a child who lives in a foreign land, then ask the class to write a story titled "My Visit with Angelo," or with another person. In their stories the children will describe life with Angelo, the weather, a few customs, the inhabitants' dress, and their amusements.

Grades 3–6
Discussing Interesting People

Ask the children to think of the most interesting person they know. Answers could include grandfather, a swimming instructor, or a next-door neighbor. Discuss the qualities that make people so fascinating or intriguing. Think of interesting words describing a person and make a list of them on the chalkboard. After the discussion, ask the class to write a paragraph using some of the words about the most interesting person they know.

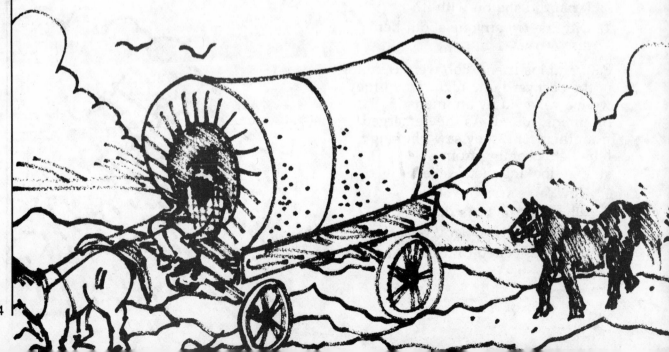

Grades 1–2
Creating Picture Stories

Write the beginning of a story on an experience chart. Draw or cut out pictures of words the children don't yet know, then ask the children to copy and complete the story, drawing or cutting out pictures of words they don't know for their stories. Four story examples follow.

This is (picture of a mother). She makes good (picture of cookies). (Tell why she makes them.)

My name is Bill. I want a (picture of a baseball bat). (Tell how well I can use it.)

My name is Karen. I have a (picture of a kitten). (Tell where it comes from.)

This is a (picture of a rabbit). He wants a (picture of a carrot). (Tell how he gets it.)

This is a (picture of a space ship). The man is an (picture of an astronaut). (Tell what he does.)

Grades 4–5
Finishing a Story

During a pioneer unit, have the children finish the following story.

During the time of the westward movement, the Carter family traveled across this vast country from Kentucky to California. Travel was very slow. They rode in a covered wagon along a trail following many other wagons. For protection, at night they made a big circle of their wagons. Sometimes, exciting and dangerous things happened to their wagon train.

Riding in the Carter wagon were Father, Mother, two-year-old Samuel, ten-year-old Roberta, and twelve-year-old Daniel. Today, as they followed the lengthy caravan through a mountain pass . . .

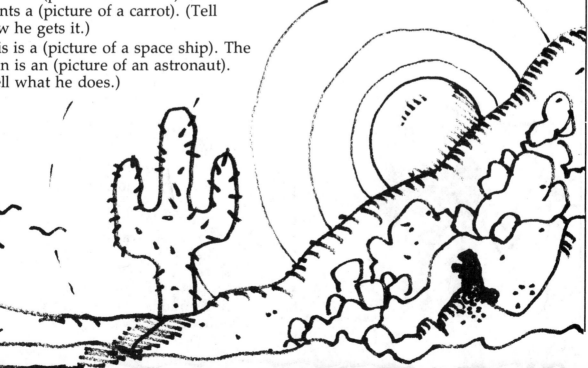

Grades 3–5
Solving a Story Situation
Ditto the following situation, leaving sufficient space for a child's answer.
Directions: Read the story.
Think of a logical solution.
Answer the question.

Returning home from school one sunny day in March, Debbie found her parents discussing the three-week spring vacation they would soon be enjoying. Debbie's collie could not go along, because they would be visiting her grandmother in Florida, who was allergic to dogs. They couldn't leave the dog in the kennel because he had gotten so lonesome the last time that he didn't eat for three days.
What would *you* do to solve Debbie's problem?

Grades 3–6
Writing New Story Endings
Ask the class to write a different ending to a folk tale, mystery, or science fiction story you have just read to them, or a story they have read that week.

Grades 4–6
Finishing a Science Fiction Thriller
Before asking the class to finish the following science fiction story, discuss the various aspects of developing a science fiction plot.

It was a hot, dull summer day with nothing to do. Jeff lounged at the base of the giant maple tree, snapping twigs and trying to think of something to do. Suddenly he heard a strange sound in the branches high above him. He was curious to find out what had made the alien noise, so he started to climb up, up, up. As he came in sight of the upper branches, he had no idea of the unusual adventure that awaited him. . . .

Grade 6
Writing about
Suggested Topics

After reading stories and information;
viewing filmstrips, films, and TV
presentations; or listening to special
radio broadcasts or recordings, give
the children specific topics to write
about. A few examples:

the World Series	Alaskan pipeline
election results	Indianapolis 500
pollution	hunger
cancer research	cheating
smoking	solar-heated homes

Grades 4–5
Writing Freedom Stories

Read to the class the book *Harriet
Tubman, Conductor of the Underground
Railway* by Ann Petry. After
discussing the book, have the children
write a story titled "What Freedom
Means to Me."

Grades 1–2
Using an Experience
Chart: Animal Adventures

Hang a large colorful picture of an
animal on the wall, changing it each
week. Write an adventure about each
animal, on an experience chart, with
the help of the class. Ask a different
child to illustrate each story. Assemble
the stories into book form. Display
the book on a chart holder for the
children to read in their leisure time.

Grades 3–5
Writing from Imagination

After reading and discussing the story
about Icarus and Daedalus (the son
and father who fashioned wings like a
bird to use as an excape from
captivity), ask the children to imagine
they can fly. Ask them how they
would feel, what they would do, and
what their lives would be like if they
were able to soar through the air. Ask
them to write a story about "My Life
As a Winged Person."

Grades 1–2
Writing "If" Stories

The help of the teacher or an aide will encourage a child to write an "If" story of his choice.

1. If you were a wild pony, what adventure might you have?
2. If you were a little lost kitten, what might happen to you?
3. If you were a little white bunny who liked to run away, what might happen to you?
4. If you were a puppy that saw a big old bull in the pasture, what might happen?
5. If you were a sleek toy boat sitting by the side of the road and it started to rain very hard, what might happen to you?
6. If you were a big red balloon and your string broke, what might happen to you?

Grades 3–5
Doing Something Nice

Tell the class about something thoughtful that one of your students did for you. What have *they* done for someone recently? Ask them to write a description of their action and illustrate it. Share their creative descriptions and illustrations by preparing a bulletin board with the title *Something Nice*. Attach their finished products to the bulletin board for display.

Grades 3–6
Being the Teacher

Plan a discussion about teaching. Children will have many questions about teacher responsibilities, among other things. Prepare to answer them in a way that will give them an understanding of the profession. At the conclusion of the discussion, suggest that each child imagine he is the teacher for the following day. Ask the class to write a story describing their day.

Grades 3–6
Making Friends

Encourage a class discussion about how to make friends: how the students became acquainted with their friends, how each one would feel if he were a new member of the class, and what it would be like to be unable to speak English in a new class. Ask each person to write a description of how he would make friends with a new student who could not speak English. Ask the class: What would you say? What would you do? How would you learn to communicate with this person?

Grades 3–6
Creating "Just-So" Stories

Choose a story to read to your class from *Just-So Stories* written by Rudyard Kipling, perhaps "How the Camel Got His Hump." Talk about the farfetched humorous nonsense. Tell the class that these stories explain why something happened. The class can write their own "Just-So" stories. Some possible ideas include:

Why Mice Have Long Tails
Why Snow Is White
How the Kangaroo Got Its Pouch
Why the Peacock Has a Beautiful Tail
How a Banana Got Its Shape
Children think of many other interesting story titles.

Variation: Insect Stories
Read a few poems about a variety of insects and review a "Just-So" story by Kipling. Spend some time discussing possibilities for writing a "Just-So" story about an insect. Children may suggest such titles as:

How the Caterpillar Became Furry
Why the Cricket Learned to Jump and Chirp
How the Wasp Got Its Stinger
How the Walking Stick Got Its Name

Grades 4–5
Writing Pioneer Stories

Write a pioneer story about your trip by covered wagon to Oregon. Include in the story some adventures such as:

1. While going through a heavy rainstorm, your wagon wheel becomes mired in the mud.

2. Upon awakening one morning, you find a small sack of money under your wagon. Explain how it got there and the events following your discovery.

3. Your covered-wagon caravan meets a small band of Indians.

4. Describe the scenery and the weather as you travel westward from Missouri to Oregon. (Use of a diary would be an interesting way to present this topic.)

5. You come to a wide, deep river. Describe how you get across.

Grades 3–6
Writing Kite Stories

During the kite-flying season, have the children pretend they are kites. Talk about possibilities of kite adventures. Ask for kite-flying words with such questions as:

1. How does a kite go? (dances, soars, flies, dives, floats, wiggles)
2. What does a kite see? (fluffy marshmallow clouds, ribbon roads and rivers, toothpick trees, roofs of many colors, clothes flapping fretfully or lazily on a clothesline, birds soaring)
3. How does the kite feel? (frightened, lonely, lazy, excited, tall, surprised)
4. Where does the kite go?
5. What happens to the kite?

After writing the words and phrases on the board, have the children write their own kite adventures.

Grades 3–4
Writing Pet Stories

Display pictures of pets on the bulletin board. Ask the children to choose a pet and write a story about it by imagining that the pet is about to become involved in a very courageous act.

Grades 3–5
Writing Bear Stories

Read a story to the class about a bear, then discuss bears in the wilderness and in zoos. Ask what would happen if a bear came to their school. After the discussion, ask the class to write a story using the following topic sentence: One day a bear came to our school. They should explain what happens in the story, who was there, and how it ends.

Grades 4–6
Writing Space Stories

Have the children read a variety of fiction and nonfiction stories and books about space. A few classroom library offerings for multilevel reading include "Operation Time Search" by André Norton, "The Best New Thing" by Isaac Asimov, "The Time Machine" and "The Invisible Man," both by H. G. Wells, "Space Cat" by Ruthven Todd, "A Wrinkle in Time" by Madeline L'Engle, and "Miss Pickerell Goes to Mars" by Ellen MacGregor. Before they create their own stories about outer space, list the space vocabulary offered by the children on an experience chart. Discuss the meaning and use of these words before starting. Allow several days for writing these stories. The class can illustrate several parts of the stories and construct sturdy covers. Display the stories on the library shelf for the children to read.

For those children who need ideas to get them started on writing an adventure in space, the teacher can make some suggestions.

1. Suppose that an astronaut finds a cave on the moon that leads to a huge cavern. Describe what he discovers and what happens to him.

2. Suppose that a spaceship from another planet has landed on the moon. Two American astronauts see it. What happens?

3. Suppose scientists develop a colony on the moon. You are among the first people chosen to live there with your family. Describe the way you live and your adventures there.

4. Suppose you are one of the astronauts chosen to visit the closest star in our galaxy. Describe your observations on the way there and explain what happens when you finally arrive years later.

Grades 3–5
Writing Dinosaur Stories

Upon returning to the classroom after a visit to the museum, discuss the life of one or two dinosaurs you saw there. Ask the class how each person felt standing next to the gigantic framework of bones. Have them imagine that the huge creature comes to life and write a story of a dinosaur's adventure in the city.

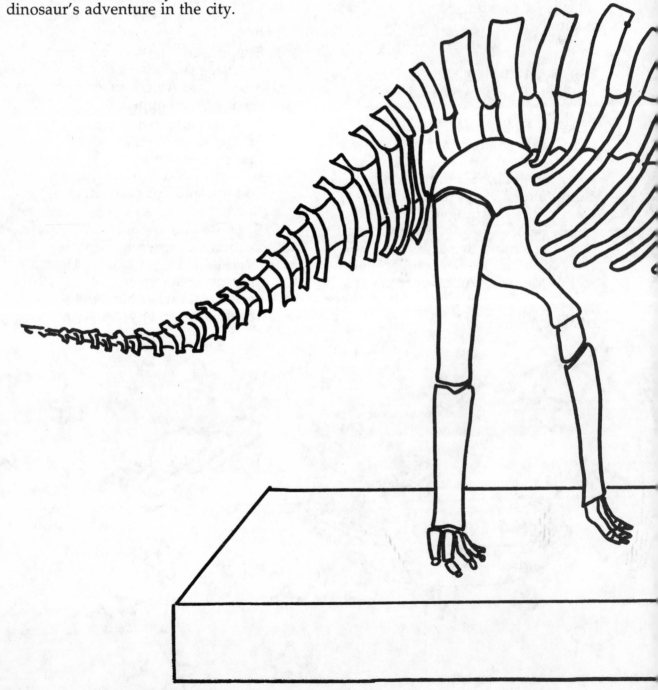

Grades 3–6
Writing and Illustrating
a Story

Have the children cut out pictures from various magazines. They can place several of the scenes or happenings in a sequence to depict certain events in a story. Using a long piece of fold-out shelfpaper, the child writes his own story from the action of the pictures and glues the pictures to the paper in appropriate places.

Grades 4–6
Writing Vacation Stories

When the students bring the Sunday paper travel section to school, ask them to read the vacation advertisements for descriptive words and phrases. Record these words on a chart so that the class can use them to write their own vacation stories.

Grades 3–5
Writing Forest Stories

Read some poems or a story to the class with woods or forest as a background. Ask the children to write a story or poem titled "A Walk Through the Woods." Illustrations add interest.

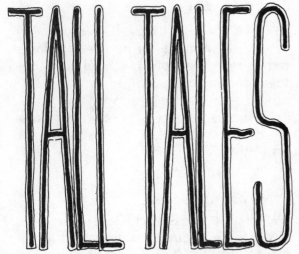

Grades 3–5
Writing Tall Tales

After reading some tall tales about Paul Bunyan, John Henry, or Pecos Bill, help the children develop their own characterizations by getting them to describe their character by appearance (size, clothing, color of hair and eyes, etc.) and sound of voice. Decide on a name. Follow with events or happenings that might occur. Record these ideas on a chart like the one that follows and let the children use them to develop their own stories.

Size? So small that she could take a bath in a thimble.

Hair? Her hair looks like yellow cotton candy.

Dress? Her dress is made from the petals of a daisy.

Voice? Her voice is as delicate as the song of a hummingbird.

Name? Thimberella

What Happened? She got locked in Mother's sewing basket.
    or
She was taking a bath in a thimble.
    or
A cat came by and put his paw on the basket.

Grades 1–3
Writing Stories by Direction

Read the story "Blaze and the Forest Fire" by C. W. Anderson to a class of first, second, or third graders. Discuss the fire and how it may have started. Ask third graders to write their own stories about a forest fire. To help them get started, use this topic sentence: One day there was a terrible forest fire.

Instead of individual stories, first and second graders might create a class story for the teacher to record on chart paper. Ask the children the following questions. They will include their answers in their story.

1. Who shall we include in our story?
2. Where will the story take place?
3. What happens?
4. When does it happen and to whom?
5. Why do these things happen?
6. How does the story end?

Grades 3–6
Writing Stories Using Newspaper Headlines

Record on the chalkboard interesting newspaper headlines that the children have brought to school. Each person chooses a headline that interests him, then creates a story supporting it. Some examples of intriguing headlines are

Smoke Traps Two Children
Girl Rescued From Subway Tracks
Storm Rages
Debris Sighted

After they have written their stories, fifth and sixth graders will enjoy acting as newscasters and tape-record them.

Grades 3–6
Writing a Structured
Story with Headings

At the top of a long sheet of shelfpaper, record the headings Male Characters, Female Characters, Animals, Time, Situations, and Type of Story. Elicit about twelve ideas from the children for each heading. For example, to get a character, ask "If you are going to write a story, who will be in it?" Continue this type of questioning for each heading. Number each idea 1 through 12. Have the children spin a dial or use dice, choosing a number at random from each section, then ask the children to write a story using these ideas. An alternate plan is to allow each child to choose an idea from each category because of his individual preference, then write a story. An example of the categories with five ideas under each heading follows:

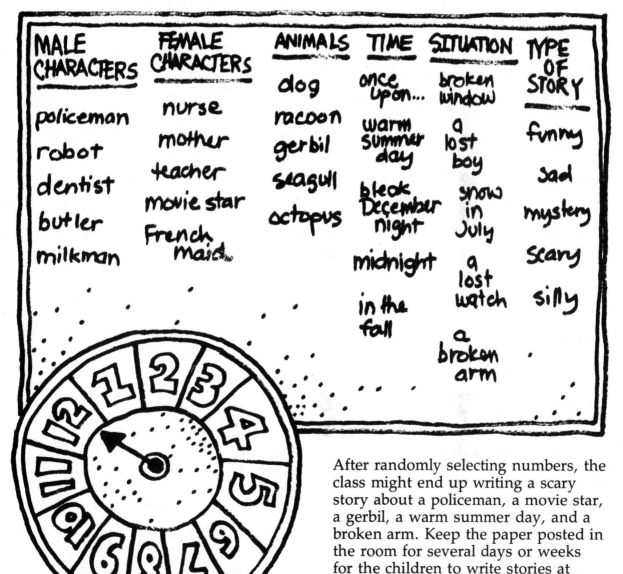

MALE CHARACTERS	FEMALE CHARACTERS	ANIMALS	TIME	SITUATION	TYPE OF STORY
policeman	nurse	dog	once upon...	broken window	funny
robot	mother	racoon	warm summer day	a lost boy	sad
dentist	teacher	gerbil	bleak December night	snow in July	mystery
butler	movie star	seagull	midnight	a lost watch	scary
milkman	French maid	octopus	in the fall	a broken arm	silly

After randomly selecting numbers, the class might end up writing a scary story about a policeman, a movie star, a gerbil, a warm summer day, and a broken arm. Keep the paper posted in the room for several days or weeks for the children to write stories at their leisure.

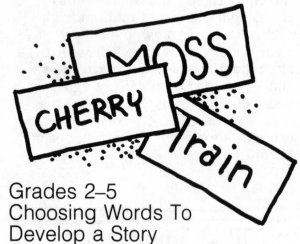

Grades 2–5
Choosing Words To
Develop a Story

Make a list on the chalkboard of at least twenty-five words offered by the class. Ask them to choose three of the words from which to develop a sentence, paragraph, or story. Differ the activity the next time by asking each child to write three different words on three slips of paper. Place the slips of paper in a shoebox, mix them, then ask each child in turn to choose any three words from the shoebox and try to use the words in a sentence, poem, paragraph, or short story.

Grades 3–6
Group-writing
Structured Stories

Divide the class into three or four groups. Have the first person in each group write a sentence on a subject of interest such as space, pioneers, Indians, spring, teachers, boys, girls, parents, and others. That person passes his sentence to the next person in the group, who must write the second sentence. Continue until each person has added a sentence. Ask each group to read its finished story to the class.

Grades 3–5
Using Another Author's Style

The children can use an author's style of writing to structure a story of their own. Read the story "Fortunately" by Remy Charlip. Then ask the children to try using a similar style by beginning each paragraph of their own stories with the words fortunately or unfortunately.

Grades 3–6
Finding Story Ideas

Have the children write about some unusual things such as alleys, windows, fences, or doors. The whole class or each child can research one of the ideas by taking a neighborhood walk, observing the various windows, fences, and doors, taking pictures, or making sketches for their word descriptions. Others might even go further and write "My Book of Doors," using cardboard or oaktag for their door-shaped cover.

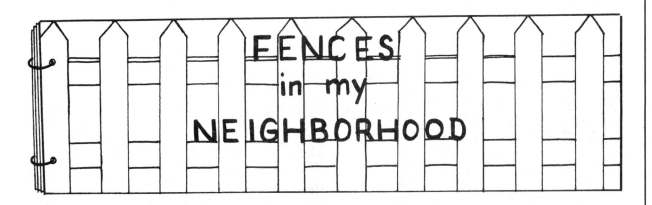

FENCES
in my
NEIGHBORHOOD

A brown split-rail fence surrounds the yard next door. Climbing roses grow on it.

My
Book
of
Doors

This is called a panel door. Mr. Best painted it red to go with his brick colonial home.

Grades 1–6
Writing First Snow Stories

The first time it snows in the fall or winter, read the story "White Snow, Bright Snow" by Alvin Tresselt to grades 1-3. For grades 4-6 the teacher might show the movie "Snow." Ask the children to write their feelings about the snow or a description of the snow. Older children should use their imaginations by pretending to be lost in the snow, describing the house they build in a snowdrift, or pretending they and their family are on a trip and must stop because of a blizzard. They then tell what happens.

Grades 3–6
Finding Story Projects among Ordinary Things

Ask the children to decide on an idea for a project, perhaps something occurring in their everyday lives. Give them a few examples, but allow each child to decide for himself. Several topics are different kinds of shoes, hair, the zoo, clocks in their town, trees, and old houses. Let the children develop this as a long-term project. For example, using a camera or making sketches, the child will have pictures of all different kinds of shoes. The shape of the cover and pages of the booklet will echo the child's idea. After each picture is arranged on its page, the child will describe or write about his thoughts on each picture.

Grades 2–6
Creating a Story
from a Picture

Display a picture where everyone can see it in the classroom or give each child an interesting picture cut out of the newspaper or a magazine and backed by a colorful piece of construction paper. Tell the students to create a story from the picture. The children should include within their stories a description of what is happening in the picture, what happened before the action in the picture took place, and what they think will happen next.

Grades 2–4
Developing a Story:
Personification

Ask the children to develop a story, putting themselves in the place of the thing about which they are writing. Give them a variety of situations from which to choose.

1. You are a baby bird just hatched from an egg. Your mother feeds you. You grow each day. It is time for you to leave the nest. Write a story telling what happens to you.

2. Imagine you are a postage stamp. In your story describe where you started, where you traveled, and your final destination.

3. Pretend you are a bottle of cola. Describe in your story all the places you visit and people you see. What finally happens to you?

Grades 1–3
Writing about an
Overnight Adventure

Write an adventure about something that happened to one of the objects in the room after that object came to life during the night. An adventure or mystery story about a live animal or insect kept in the room at school is another possibility. For example, one morning the children arrived at school to find tiny, sticky eggs on desks, the floor, the windowsill, and the file cabinet. The mystery was solved when the children found the butterfly that had laid the eggs overnight. The class wrote a story about this unusual mystery on an experience chart with the help of the teacher.

139

and . . . I like
by Ada Phipps Harper

When I wake up in the morning,
    I like a little sun;
I like a little laughter, and
    I like a little fun,
and
    I like a little song that
        is very light and gay;
    I like a little tune to
        brighten up my day.
and
    I like a little friend to
        come and play with me.
    I like a little swing in
        the shade of a tree,
and
    I like a little cooky with
        a raisin hidden in it.
    (I think I'll have another
        in a very little minute.)
and
    I like the pretty colors of
        the evening's setting sun.
    I like a little story when
        my busy day is done.

From JACK AND JILL magazine, copyright © 1962 by
The Curtis Publishing Company.

Grades 1–4
Writing "I Like . . ." Stories
After reading the poem "and . . . I
like" by Ada Phipps Harper, ask third
and fourth graders to describe the
things they like by making a list,
poem, or story, using descriptive
words. Incorporate these creations
into a class booklet. First and second
graders can make a booklet with the
title "I Like . . .," each page
containing an illustration with a
description.

Grades 3–6
Interviewing a Doctor

Invite a doctor (perhaps the father of a student) to visit your room for an interview. Ask one of the children to write an invitation to include such information as when (time), where (room number and grade), and why (purpose). Ask the rest of the class to write questions that they would like to have answered during the interview.

Grades 3–6
Interviewing a Special Teacher

Invite the special education teacher from your school or another school for an interview. Discuss with the class the kind of information to be gained from such an interview, then have the children write questions that they would like to have answered. This activity will allow children to gain insight into the kinds of special problems children their own age face.

Grades 1–3
Writing Together— A Class Project

As a class project, have the children write a story together containing several chapters. Set aside a time each week for the class to add a chapter to the story, written on an experience chart. Have the class decide what kind of character they want their chapter to revolve around (for instance, a curious person like Homer Price or a tiny mouse that causes mischief). Each chapter will tell about a new adventure with the storybook character. Ask each child to draw a picture of their storybook character, then let them choose the one they want to represent the main character. Select a few children to draw illustrations for the story.

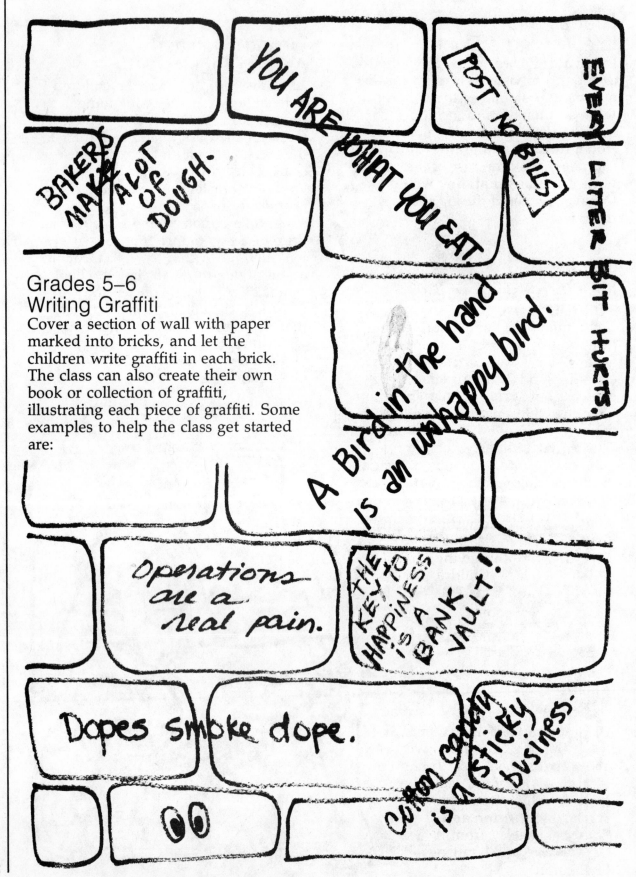

YOU ARE WHAT YOU EAT

POST NO BILS

EVERY LITTER BIT HURTS.

BAKERS MAKE

A LOT OF DOUGH.

A Bird in the hand is an unhappy bird.

Grades 5–6
Writing Graffiti

Cover a section of wall with paper marked into bricks, and let the children write graffiti in each brick. The class can also create their own book or collection of graffiti, illustrating each piece of graffiti. Some examples to help the class get started are:

Operations are a real pain.

THE KEY TO HAPPINESS IS A BANK VAULT!

Dopes smoke dope.

cotton candy is a sticky business.

Grades 3–6
Pretending in Poetry

Have the children write some pretend poetry. For instance, ask them to pretend they are a bus, a toboggan, a comb, a drinking fountain, a candle, or a library book. They should tell what happens, how they feel, and whom they meet.

Grades 5–6
Creating Iffy Books

Inspire the class to create a book or collection of "if" sentences. To get them started, give the children the following "iffy" sentences:

If I were a telephone pole, I would be stuck up.

If a crow snatched my watch, I could see time fly.

Grades 3–6
Writing Holiday Poetry

On the chalkboard write lists of words that remind the class of Halloween, Christmas, Thanksgiving, or Valentine's Day. Children associate the following words with Halloween.

witch	broom	trick
black cat	screech	treat
ghost	hoot	fun
goblin	brew	costumes
shiver	sneak	jack-o'-lantern
shake	boo-oo-oo	screams

Using these and other words, have the children create their own poems about that special day. To get the class into the mood, read them a few holiday poems from *Sing a Song of Seasons* by Brewton and the poem "October Magic" from *Whispers and Other Poems* by Myra Cohn Livingston.

Grades 4–6
Introducing the Cinquain

Lead a class discussion, explaining that the cinquain form contains five lines and generally has a 2-4-6-8-2 syllable count.

——— ———
——— ——— ——— ———
——— ——— ——— ——— ——— ———
——— ——— ——— ——— ——— ———
——— ———

To illustrate how the lines are filled in, start by naming any object, such as a turtle, that contains two syllables:

Turtle
Small, hard shell, cute
Swims fast, crawls so slowly
Green, little funny-designed shells
Tortoise.

Another form utilizes *words* in each space instead of syllables. Within this form (as used in the poem above), line 1 contains one word representing a title, line 2 contains two words describing the title, line 3 contains three words expressing action about the title, line 4 contains words expressing feeling about the title, and line 5 contains one word expressing another word for the title. For example:

Snow
White, fluffy
Falling slowly earthward
Little helpless cold things
Crystals

After discussing the cinquain and reading some examples from last year's class, ask the children to try one of the forms together. Mark the lines on the chalkboard and fill in as the children share their ideas. Have a child copy the cinquain and put it in the class poetry scrapbook. Set up both forms mentioned on experience charts and display them in the classroom so that individual children can write a cinquain at their leisure.

Grades 4–6
Introducing Haiku Poetry

The proper form for creating this kind of Japanese poetry is composed of three lines, five syllables for line 1, seven syllables for line 2, and five syllables for line 3. True Haiku poetry relates to nature, especially seasonal happenings, and expresses a perception about one idea or thought. To get the children started with a topic, show a few seasonal pictures on the opaque projector. Then make a list of things that relates to nature such as the following.

icycles   apple blossoms
bare trees   butterflies
grey skies   dandelions
wind   babbling brook
crackling ice bees
sleet   crickets
pine trees   rain
burning logs   roses
fresh air   daisies
puddles   fresh grass
pussy willows fruit trees
yellow forsythia pumpkins
bluejays   leaves
raindrops   frogs
               damp earth
               lilacs

Try creating a poem together. Have the children fill in lines placed on the chalkboard, using ideas on the list.

5   Daisy in the yard,
7   A yellow and white princess,
5   Shining in the sun.

The children may want to try writing Haiku of their own, following the class creation.

Grades 4–6
Introducing Senryu Poetry

Senryu is written in three lines with a 5-7-5 syllable count. When working with this type of poetry, any subject matter may be used. Topics are not limited to nature as in Haiku, but do contain a single idea. Set up lines on the chalkboard to represent the syllabic form. Discuss various subjects of the children's choosing and fill in the syllabic frame as the ideas develop. Choices for topics include a kitten, turtle, mushroom, blimp, planet, candle, shoes, car, and many more. An example using a kitten as the topic follows.

5   My soft gray kitten
7   Purrs, stretches, and yawns, then creeps
5   Silently away.

Let the children try doing one by themselves, after one or two group efforts.

Grades 1–6
Writing Concrete Poetry

Have the children decide on a noun, perhaps from a unit being studied. Write a description of the noun, placing the words on paper in special arrangements, each child designing his own form. For example:

Giraffe
Spotted long-necked
    Quiet swift yellow
        Tall graceful
           Long-legged
           Zoo
           Animal

Boys
Mischievous mysterious (can use some alliteration)
    Active lazy (can use opposites)
        Athletic
           Male

Other examples:

Christmas: shape of a Christmas tree
rain: shape of an umbrella
birthday party: shape of a cake and candles
sun: shape of the sun and rays
flower: shape of a flower (perhaps a daisy)
eye: shape of an eye

Variation:

Arrange a variety of real fruit in a bowl. As the children eat the fruit, ask them to think about how it feels, tastes, and looks. This exercise will arm them with data for writing concrete poetry the shape and color of the fruit. Let the children make a bulletin board display of their poetry, written as the shapes of fruit on colored construction paper arranged in a cut-out paper bowl stapled to the bulletin board.

BEAUTIFUL HOT
BRIGHT SUN BALL ORANGE

RAIN
POURS PITTER-PATTERS PELTS
DRIPS & DRENCHES
PUDDLES

CHRISTMAS
★
LOVE
BELLS
LIGHTS
PRESENTS
STOCKINGS
CANDY CANES
JESUS' BIRTHDAY
U

Birthday Party
games goodies cake candy candles children
singing Presents laughter
Prizes
fun

Grades 3–6
Creating Poetry:
"See What I Found"

Read several poems from the book *See What I Found* by Myra Cohn Livingston to the class. Provide a box full of items such as an old book, a scarf, an apple, a doll, a jar containing a dead moth, a wallet, a mirror, and other choices. Have each child write the title "See What I Found" on his paper. Everyone should take an object from the box and write what *he* has found on the first line, tell something about that object on the second line, tell where he would find such an object on the third line, tell what purpose that object has on the fourth and fifth lines, and say anything he wants to say about the object on the sixth line.

See What I Found

A book

A very old brown book

Lost in the corner
of a library shelf.

A book to balance on
my head

A book to read when
there's nothing
else to do.

Many adventures of
yesterday

Grades 3–6
Writing Poems While Listening to Music

While the children are writing poems about ice skating, play some skating music on the record player to get them into the skating mood. At the same time, use a slide projector to show a slide of a pond and skaters or display a skating scene recently created by the class on the bulletin board.

Grades 3–6
Writing Weather Poems

Read a variety of poems to the class about the seasons and weather. Poems written by other children are of interest, too. Discuss weather words, then make a list of children's suggestions.

> windy gusts
> snow crystals
> drizzling rain
> misty fog
> fog obscures
> hail ricochets
> powdery snow
> wind whistles
> wind screams
> rain batters
> scorching sun
> humid air
> swirling snow
> hail bounces
> patter of raindrops

Ask the children to use some of the words discussed and recorded, and others of their own, to write weather poems.

Grades 3–6
Writing Poems about Food

Read poems about food to the class, then write a class poem about favorite foods. Initiate interest by writing lists of favorite foods, then lists of smell, taste, color, shape, and feel words. The children will contribute lines for their poem, which does not have to rhyme. Use a similar format for other areas of interest: a spring day, a summer picnic, a camping trip, a forest fire, Thanksgiving dinner, a baby sister.

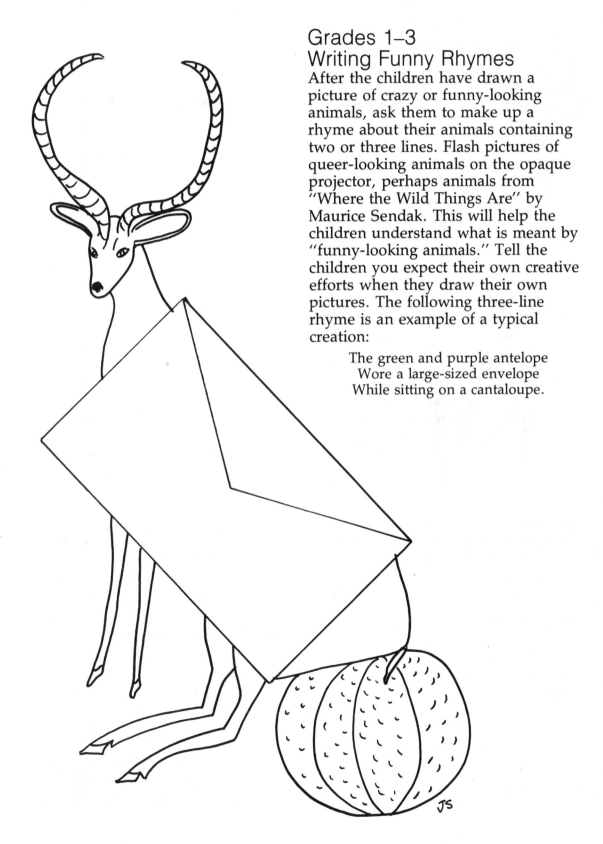

Grades 1–3
Writing Funny Rhymes

After the children have drawn a picture of crazy or funny-looking animals, ask them to make up a rhyme about their animals containing two or three lines. Flash pictures of queer-looking animals on the opaque projector, perhaps animals from "Where the Wild Things Are" by Maurice Sendak. This will help the children understand what is meant by "funny-looking animals." Tell the children you expect their own creative efforts when they draw their own pictures. The following three-line rhyme is an example of a typical creation:

> The green and purple antelope
> Wore a large-sized envelope
> While sitting on a cantaloupe.

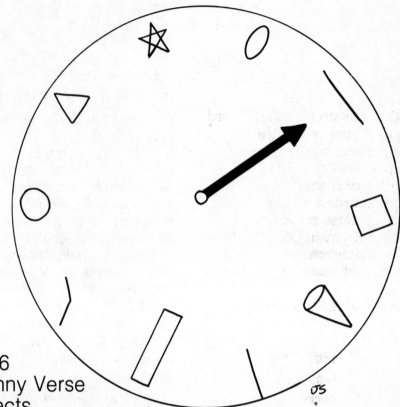

Grades 3–6
Writing Funny Verse
about Objects

Draw the following objects on a piece of circular oaktag: a star, a horizontal line, an oval, a triangle, a cylinder, a perpendicular line, a square, a slanted line, a circle, and a rectangle. With a brad fastener connect an arrow to the middle of the circle. The children can dial an object. Ask them to use imagination when looking at the object dialed and then write a funny verse about it. A perpendicular line poem is:

> This telephone
> pole holds
> tightly to wires
> that get news
> to firemen to
> put out fires.

Thinking about a horizontal line brings forth:

> As a window sill
> I can sit quite still
> Too much dust on me makes me ill.

Accompany the verse with the figure drawing.

Grades 4–6
Introducing Limericks

Read some limericks to the class. Ask them to write a few of their own using humorous or unusual-sounding city names with their verses. Give the class road maps of all the states. They will discover many town and city names by using the maps. To get the class started, use a few of the following names: Beanblossom, Chugwater, Nanty Glo, Mahwah. Try one.

> There was a young lad from Beanblossom
> Who ate dozens of doughnuts and then
> some,
> His pants got so tight
> And try as he might,
> He couldn't continue to eat some.

Grades 4–6
Rhyming

Write several words on the chalkboard for the class to rhyme with others such as elastic, fairy, blister, ocean, delighted, and collision. With class help, make a list of rhyming words for each word recorded on the chalkboard. Each class member can select one set of rhyming words to create a poem. Sometimes the verse will be serious, and sometimes quite funny.

A possible list of rhyming words follows.

elastic	fairy
plastic	wary
drastic	carry
mystic	marry
futuristic	hairy

collision
division
derision
incision
precision

ocean	blister
motion	mister
notion	sister
potion	Lister
devotion	kissed 'er

Example of a rhymed verse using the word delighted:

My sis was not delighted
When her new dress ignited
She became so excited
That she yelled for brother Ted.
He ignored her, she felt slighted
Her dress became so blighted.

Grades 2–6
Relating Poems to Arts and Crafts

Children can relate their original poetry to art experiences. Provide materials needed for drawing, painting, sketching, sculpturing, sewing and making dioramas, papier-mâché objects, and puppets. These materials should be easily accessible to children:

tongue depressors
scissors
wheat paste
strips of old
    newspapers
cotton
magazines
material and
    sewing notions
shoeboxes and
    smaller boxes
manila drawing
    paper
colored construction
    paper
paints and brushes
pencils
pastels
crayons
clay

Highlight the poetry and illustrations as displays on bulletin boards, shelves, tables, the backs of pianos and dividers, and hanging mobiles. Utilize your window shades for displaying poems, art work, and drawings. Masking tape folded behind each corner of a drawing leaves no marks on the shades. The shades can still be easily raised and lowered.

Grades 1–6
Writing Letters

There are many natural opportunities for writing letters. When the class is inviting the principal, fire chief, or a local doctor for an interview, collect ideas orally and write them on the chalkboard. Choose a child in the lower grades to copy the letter. Have an older child compose his own letter from ideas listed on the board. A day or two following an interview or field trip experience, ask each child to compose his own thank-you letter, including an idea or two that the child genuinely liked about the experience or about something that he learned.

Other real opportunities for writing letters are to ask permission to accompany the class on a field trip; letters of convalescence; requests for information; and letters to pen pals, grandparents, a good friend who moved away, or a favorite author.

During social studies class after the study of various historical events, have George Washington write to his wife, Martha, Meriwether Lewis to George Rogers Clark, and Ben Franklin to Thomas Jefferson. Other unique letters children enjoy writing are Grandmother sending a message to Red Riding Hood, a bat's letter to a baseball, a saucer writing to a cup. Children will think of others.

Grades 3–6
Making a Weekly Newspaper

A bulletin board newspaper for the third and fourth grades and a dittoed newspaper for the fifth and sixth grades would keep the students up-to-date with current news happenings in the world as well as in the classroom. Let the class decide upon a title and the various sections of the newspaper. Some topics to include are Trips, Class News, World News, Special Events, Weather, The Comics, Riddles, Poetry, Spotlight on People, Artist of the Week, Lost and Found, Jokes, Best Books, and Sports News.

Grades 3–6
Keeping Diaries

Diaries for classroom use are easy and fun for children, practical as well as creative. Perhaps third graders could keep a daily account of an imaginary pioneer family moving from Missouri, travelling over the Rocky Mountains to California. Each day a different child will write an exciting account to add to the class diary.

A fourth-grade class might write a diary of daily happenings as a modern-day family drives across the United States from New York to California, describing what they see as they move from one area to the next: topography, products grown, manufacturing, size of cities, size of farms, and many other features. Fifth or sixth graders could keep a daily diary about a trip through their own home state, describing interesting land forms, state parks, cities, agricultural products grown, manufacturing, special features, and other things.

THE DAILY NEWS

CLASS NEWS

ARTIST OF THE WEEK

WORLD NEWS

LOST AND FOUND

RIDDLES

POETRY

SPOTLIGHT ON PEOPLE

SPECIAL EVENTS

JOKES

WEATHER

COMICS

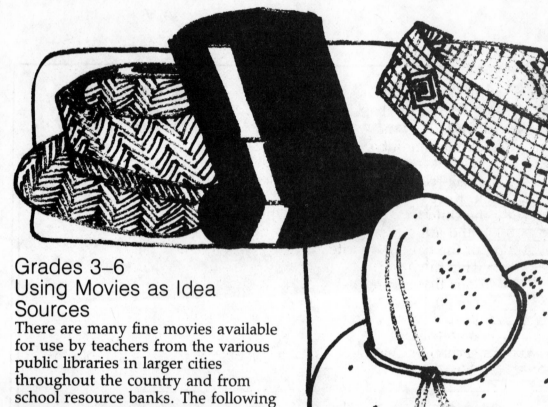

Grades 3–6
Using Movies as Idea Sources

There are many fine movies available for use by teachers from the various public libraries in larger cities throughout the country and from school resource banks. The following list of movie titles is especially useful for creative writing experiences.

Rainshower	The Waterfalls
Pigs	Winter Geyser
Fiddle DeDee	Sky Above
Clay	Clown
Snow	

After viewing the movie, discuss and describe the scenes, action, sounds, colors, and characters. The children might like to describe what they saw or heard by writing a story, a sentence, a paragraph, or a poem (concrete, cinquain, or rhymed verse). The movie could be used to introduce a discussion of similes and metaphors. As the movie is being viewed, stop the projector occasionally and ask the class to write a sentence describing the waterfall, the geyser, or the sky. After the viewing, ask the class to think of words describing the waterfall. Write the descriptive words on a chart for display so that the class can use them when writing their creative stories or poems.

Grades 1–2
Making a Bulletin Board of Hats and Comments

During a unit about community helpers, have each child draw a hat belonging to someone in the community such as the policeman, fireman, baker, butcher, and nurse. Each child will dictate comments of the special person wearing the hat, while the teacher writes beneath each drawing. Set up a bulletin board display with the variety of hats.

Grades 2–4
Making a Book Report Display

A bulletin board display titled *Blast Off to Bookland* will give the children in class the incentive to read many books. The child should fill out a dittoed sheet and give it to the teacher so that he will receive credit for reading a book. Keep the ditto simple. Require the child's name, the name of the book and author, and a short description of the child's favorite part of the book. This can also be done orally at various times of the day. Use tally marks on a chart of children's names posted near the bulletin board to keep track of the number of books each child reads.

On the bulletin board, place a cut-out portion of the curve of the earth's surface, and on this, place cut-out rockets with a child's name on each one. On the rest of the bulletin board space, strategically place five round-shaped planets with the words *five books, ten books, fifteen books, twenty books,* and *thirty books*. The children can make up names for each planet. The largest planet with *thirty books* printed on it should be named Bookland. When a child has read five books he can move his rocket to the planet that says *five books* on it. Short straight-pins with colored beads at the end work best for keeping the rockets in place, and the children can also move them easily to the next planet as they increase the number of books read.

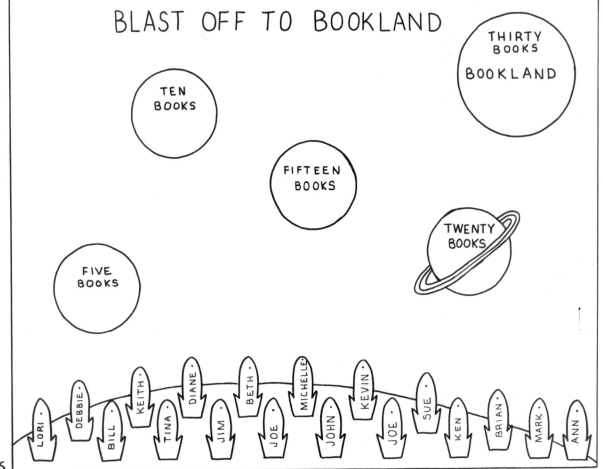

Grades 3–6
Using Personification

After the reading of stories using personification (*Bambi*, Felix Salten; *Hitty, Her First Hundred Years*, Rachel Field; *Charlotte's Web*, E. B. White), have the children write an adventure or an incident about a doorknob, leaf, teardrop, pair of canvas shoes, rag doll, gym teacher's whistle, ladder, or baseball. The children will think of others. Explain that the object must assume lifelike characteristics—talk, move, feel, see, and smell.

Display an old pair of gym shoes, ballet slippers, a fireman's hat, a snorkel and mask, or a thermometer, and ask the class to write a story using personification about the thing being displayed.

Ask the children to write riddles about objects such as a match, pencil, toast, eraser, hamburger, or dill pickle, describing characteristics of that object as if it were alive. For example, in writing a riddle about a match, someone might describe it in the following way: "Ouch! Someone just scratched my head real hard! Help! My head is on fire!" Who am I?

Grades 3–6
Describing the
Main Character

Have the children write a description of the main character of a book that you have just read to them. Allowing the use of a variety of art materials of their choosing, ask the class to create a picture character from their descriptions. Using pipe cleaners, cloth, construction paper, and a shoebox, they might construct a diorama. Modeling clay might be used to sculpture a character, or a child might choose to use crayons, paint, or pastels on drawing paper. An ice-cream stick or tongue depressor clothed with cotton balls and cloth could represent a puppet caricature of the character. Display the art work along with the written descriptions. Each child's concept of the story character will show some interesting comparisons.

Grades 3–5
Using Personification in Conversations

Use the following ideas for conversations as a creative writing activity or role playing activity:

1. What does your sandwich say to the apple inside your lunch box?

2. What do your gym shoes talk about at night after everyone has left the school?

3. What are the oranges saying to the apples as they sit in the refrigerator ready to be eaten?

4. What do your two pet gerbils talk about at night when everyone else is asleep?

5. What might the tall redwood tree say to the young pine tree?

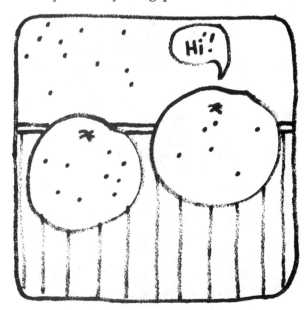

Grades 3–6
Writing Personification Using Humorous Monologue

The children will enjoy writing humorous monologues involving wallets belonging to well-known people. Include places visited, items put into the wallet, money spent, perhaps a pickpocket adventure, or being lost. Tell what happens.

Grades 3–5
Personifying Christmas Objects

The Christmas season provides many opportunities for writing stories using personification. The children could personify a Christmas stocking, a Christmas tree, presents, or the angel on top of the Christmas tree. Talk about how the angel feels being placed on top of the tree. What does she see? Where would she rather be, or is she satisfied with her position? Does she have any fears? Does she like the family? What are some interesting daily happenings she might observe? After using the guided discussion format, invite the children to write a story about one of the objects, using personification.

Grades 3–6
Using Pictures
To Study Personification

Have the class cut out pictures of various objects such as different kinds of chairs. Ask, "What are these chairs saying to each other? How do they feel when adults, children, and pets sit on them?" Ask each person to write a sentence or two about each picture as if he were the object.

Grades 3–6
Personifying Insects

Call several children to the chalkboard to write the names of insects they know, each child in the class choosing the name of an insect to impersonate, then writing a letter home about what happened last week. A child may choose to write about the insect playing baseball, the problem of getting to work each day, buying groceries, keeping house, buying presents, or having a conversation with another insect.

Discuss one or two Superman adventures, then ask the children to write a tall tale or adventure story about a brave and fearless Superinsect.

Grades 2–4
Picturing Yourself

Ask the children to imagine how they looked as a baby, then draw a self-portrait. Then tell them to write a sentence or paragraph describing what they were doing. Have the children imagine how they will look when they get their first job, then draw a picture. They should describe in a paragraph the kind of work they are doing. Accompany this activity with the reading of the poems "John Plans" by Dorothy Mason Pierce and "When I Grow Up" by William Wise, from the book *Birthday Candles Burning Bright* by Sara and John Brewton.

Grades 2–5
Choosing a Child of the Week

Every Friday choose a child in class as child of the week. The child selected gathers materials about himself over the weekend with the help of his family. On Monday he arranges his materials on the bulletin board. He can bring in such materials as photographs, pictures, and drawings, then write sentences or paragraphs describing the photographs and events in his life.

Grades 3–6
Telling "All about Myself"

Begin a discussion about the things that make one a special person such as a child's own special features. Ask for things he especially likes and dislikes and things that make him happy and sad. Following the discussion the class can write paragraphs describing the things that make each one a special person. Using a mirror, the child can draw a picture of himself and attach it to his paragraph. Use this activity as one of the chapters in a book that the children will write, *All About Myself.* For other chapters include a one-page autobiography, baby pictures, stories, poems, and special lists containing favorite foods, books, places to visit, and so on.

Grades 3–6
Writing Autobiographies

Ask the class to interview their parents to answer the following questions about themselves:

Where was I born?

What kind of day or night was it?

What was my favorite toy as a baby?

Did I ever have any accidents or get hurt in some way? At what age?

Did I ever visit any interesting places when I was a baby?

Add any other information you wish.

Choose a title of your choice.

Bring a baby snapshot of yourself to school.

A follow-up activity of interest to the class is to locate the birthplace of each child on a large outline of a United States map. Mark each spot with a colored straight-pin to hold each name in place. Make a class notebook or create a bulletin board display with the snapshots and stories.

Grades 1–6
Displaying Baby Pictures

Arrange a large bulletin board with baby pictures of each child in class. This activity provides a lot of fun for the children as they try to guess whom the baby picture represents.

Grades 3–6
Discussing Family Life

After a class discussion about the various roles of family members, arguments that sometimes occur, task sharing, and other things, ask the children to write a paragraph about things he can do to help matters run smoothly at home.

Grades 3–5
Discussing Relatives

Discuss with the children what their fathers, mothers, grandmothers, grandfathers, sisters, or brothers are like. Talk about things they do together and how they feel about their relatives. Invite them to write a paragraph about (a) Things I Like about My Father (or other relatives mentioned) or (b) Things I Like to Do with My Father (or others mentioned).

Grades 2–4
Discussing Childhood Fears

Discuss inner fears that children have, the teacher sharing some of her own fears as a child. Read the story "There's a Nightmare in My Closet" by Mercer Mayer. Talk about how one's imagination can magnify fears. Ask each person to write about something that frightens him.

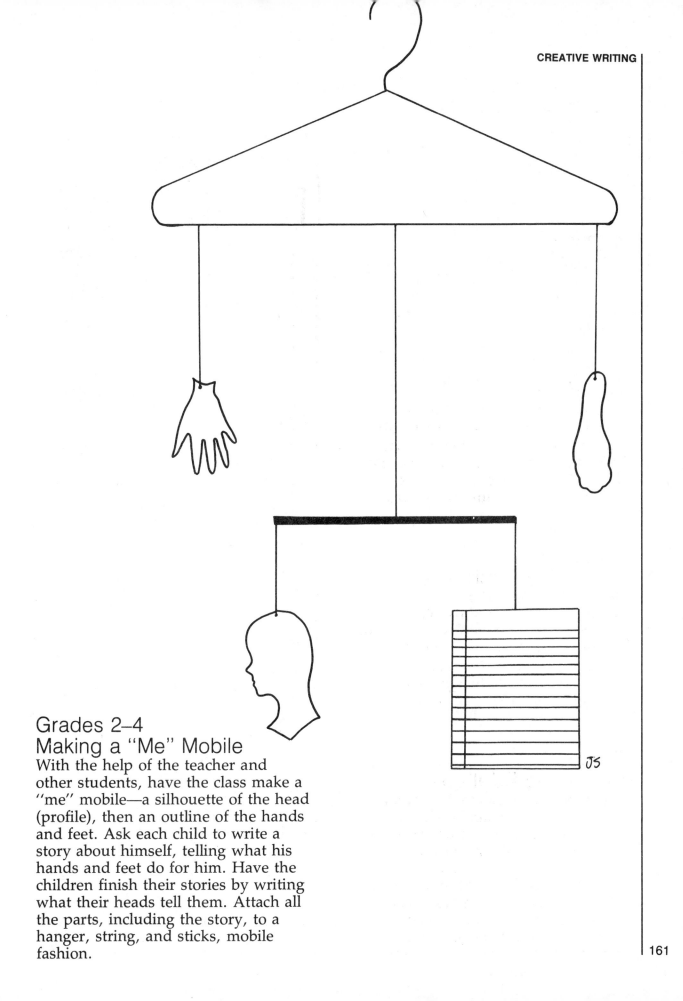

Grades 2–4
Making a "Me" Mobile

With the help of the teacher and other students, have the class make a "me" mobile—a silhouette of the head (profile), then an outline of the hands and feet. Ask each child to write a story about himself, telling what his hands and feet do for him. Have the children finish their stories by writing what their heads tell them. Attach all the parts, including the story, to a hanger, string, and sticks, mobile fashion.

Grades 3–5
Writing Riddles: Self-concept

At Halloween time the children can write riddles describing themselves, ending with the line "Who-oo-oo am I?" Attach these riddles to a ghost, witch, bat, or pumpkin puppet made by each pupil and displayed on a bulletin board. The children have fun guessing each other's riddles.

Grades 3–6
Collecting Stories and Poems

Certain students who are interested should help their teacher organize stories, poems, and other creative writings collected from each child in the class. Reproduce the collection later as a booklet for each person. At the beginning of the school year, place a large manila envelope or folder in a conspicuous spot to collect at least one good creative writing effort of each child in the class. The teacher will have to be the judge of what is put into the envelope. A committee of students will organize the material, then print it on dittoes to be run off by the teacher. Conduct a contest among students for an illustrated cover for the booklet. The children can act as judges to choose their favorite picture, and the teacher will ditto the winning drawing and run it off on thin, colored construction paper. Students will help assemble the booklet pages and cover. Give each class member a booklet during the last week of school to read, enjoy, and collect autographs.

Grades 5–6
Discussing Pet Peeves

Carry on a class discussion about things that irritate each person. Talk about ways these bothersome things can be reconciled. Suggest that they each write a list of their pet peeves and include suggestions for reducing or eliminating each one. Read the following poem to start them thinking.

I Don't Like *Don't*—I Don't, I Don't!
by Lucia and James L. Hymes, Jr.

I hear a million *don'ts* a day.
No matter what I do they say . . .
   Now don't do this,
   And don't do that,
   Don't interrupt,
   Don't tease the cat.
   Don't bite your nails,
   Don't slam the door,
   Don't leave those messes on the floor.
   Don't shout,
   Don't fight,
   Don't spill your food.
   Now don't talk back
   And don't be rude.
   Don't let the dog climb on your bed,
   And don't forget what I just said.
   Don't track in mud,
   Don't slip,
   Don't run.
   Don't lose your cap,
   Don't point that gun.
   Don't touch the tray,
   Don't tear your clothes,
   And don't forget to blow your nose.
   Don't go too far,
   Don't climb that tree,
   And don't fall down and skin your knee.
I don't like *don't* one little bit.
Look! Now they've got *me* saying it!

BIBLIOGRAPHY:
Part Four

Anderson, C. W. *Blaze and the Forest Fire.* New York: The Macmillan Company, 1964.

Asimov, Isaac. *The Best New Thing.* New York: William Collins Sons & Company, Ltd., 1971.

Blassingame, Wyatt. *Pecos Bill Rides a Tornado.* Champaign, Illinois: Garrard Publishing Company, 1973.

Brewton, Sara. *Sing A Song of Seasons.* New York: The Macmillan Company, 1955.

Brewton, Sara and John. *Birthday Candles Burning Bright.* New York: The Macmillan Company, 1960.
Poems–"John Plans," Dorothy Mason Pierce
    "When I Grow Up," William Wise

Charlip, Remy. *Fortunately.* New York: Parents Magazine Press, 1949.

Conford, Ellen. *Why Can't I Be William?* Boston: Little, Brown, & Company, 1972.

Felton, Harold W. *Pecos Bill and the Mustang.* Englewood Cliffs, New Jersey: Prentice-Hall, Inc., 1965.

Field, Rachel. *Hitty, Her First Hundred Years.* New York: The Macmillan Company, 1931.

Fleischman, Sid. *Longbeard the Wizard.* Boston: Little, Brown, & Company, 1970.

Johnson, Edna; Scott, Carrie E.; and Sickels, Evelyn R. *Anthology of Children's Literature.* Boston: Houghton Mifflin Company, 1970.
Greek Myth–"Icarus and Daedalus"

Keeping, Charles. *Joseph's Yard.* New York: Franklin Watts, Inc., 1969.

Kipling, Rudyard. *Just-So Stories.* Garden City, New York: Doubleday & Company, 1912.
Story–"How the Camel Got His Hump"

Konigsburg, Elaine. *From the Mixed-up Files of Mrs. Basil E. Frankweiler.* New York: Atheneum Publishers, 1972.

L'Engle, Madeline. *A Wrinkle in Time.* New York: Ariel Books, 1962.

Livingston, Myra Cohn. *Whispers and Other Poems.* New York: Harcourt, Brace & Company, 1958.
Poem–"October Magic"

Livingston, Myra Cohn and Blegvad, Erik. *See What I Found.* New York: Harcourt Brace Jovanovich, 1962.

MacGregor, Ellen. *Miss Pickerell Goes to Mars.* New York: Whittlesey House, McGraw-Hill Book Company, 1951.

Martin, Bill Jr. *Little Princess Goodnight.* New York: Kinder-Owl Books: Literature Series, Holt, Rinehart, & Winston, Inc., 1971.

Mayer, Mercer. *There's a Nightmare in My Closet.* New York: The Dial Press, 1968.

McCormick, Dell J. *Paul Bunyan Swings His Ax.* New York: Caxton Printers, 1936, Scholastic Book Services, 1963.

Norton, André. *Operation Time Search.* New York: Harcourt, Brace & Company, 1967.

O'Neill, Mary. *Fingers Are Always Bringing Me News.* Garden City, New York: Doubleday & Company, 1969.

—————. *Hailstones and Halibut Bones.* Garden City, New York: Doubleday & Company, 1961.

—————. *What Is That Sound!* New York: Atheneum Publishers, 1966.

Petry, Ann. *Harriet Tubman, Conductor of the Underground Railway.* New York: Thomas Y. Crowell, 1955.

Salten, Felix. *Bambi.* New York: Simon & Schuster, Inc., 1970.

Sendak, Maurice. *Where the Wild Things Are.* New York: Harper & Row Publishers, 1963.

Shephard, Esther. *Paul Bunyan.* New York: Harcourt, Brace & Company, 1941.

Stein, R. *Steel Driving Men; the Legend of John Henry.* Chicago: Children's Press, 1969.

Thayer, Ernest. *Casey at the Bat.* New York: Franklin Watts, Inc., 1964.

Thayer, Jane. *What's A Ghost Going to Do?* New York: William Morrow & Company, 1966.

Todd, Ruthven. *Space Cat.* New York: Charles Scribner's Sons, 1952.

Tresselt, Alvin. *White Snow, Bright Snow.* New York: Lothrop, Lee, & Shepard Company, Inc., 1947.

Wells, H. G. *The Invisible Man.* New York: Airmont Publishing Company, Inc., 1964.

—————. *Time Machine.* New York: Airmont Publishing Company, Inc., 1964.

White, E. B. *Charlotte's Web.* New York: Harper & Row Publishers, Inc., 1952.

FILM REFERENCES: Part Four

Clay. 10 minutes, black & white, 1964. Produced and distributed by Image Resources, New York.

Clown. 15 minutes, color, 1969. Produced and distributed by Learning Corporation of America, New York.

Fiddle De Dee. 4 minutes, color, 1948. Produced by National Film Board of Canada, New York. Distributed by International Film Bureau, Chicago.

Pigs. 11 minutes, color, 1967. Produced by Dimension Films, Los Angeles. Distributed by Churchill Films, Los Angeles.

Rainshower. 15 minutes, color, 1965. Produced by Dimension Films, Los Angeles. Distributed by Churchill Films, Los Angeles.

Sky Above. 10 minutes, color, 1970. Produced by David Adams, Santa Monica, California. Distributed by Pyramid Films, Santa Monica, California.

Snow. 13 minutes, color, 1962. Produced by National Film Board of Canada (U.S. in New York). Distributed by BFA Educational Media, Santa Monica, California.

The Waterfalls. 12 minutes, black and white. Produced and Distributed by Pictura Films, New York.

Winter Geyser. 7 minutes, color, 1968. Produced and Distributed by Pyramid Films, Santa Monica. California.